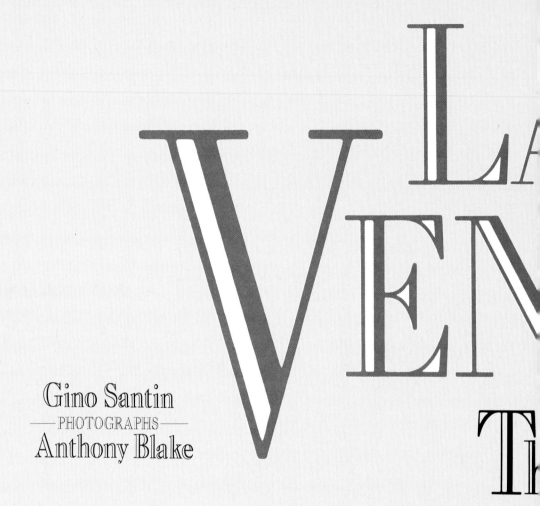

Gino Santin
—PHOTOGRAPHS—
Anthony Blake

CUCINA VENEZIANA

Food & cooking of Venice

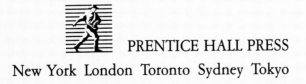

PRENTICE HALL PRESS

New York London Toronto Sydney Tokyo

Prentice Hall Press
15 Columbus Circle
New York, New York 10023

First impression 1988

Originally published in Great Britain in 1988 by Ebury Press

PRENTICE HALL PRESS and colophon are registered trademarks
of Simon & Schuster Inc.

Library of Congress Catalog Card Number: 89 – 60710
ISBN: 0–13–521816–0

10 9 8 7 6 5 4 3 2 1
First Prentice Hall Press Edition

Editor: Susan Fleming
Designer: Harry Green

The Publishers would like to thank Elizabeth David Ltd, 46 Bourne Street,
London SW1 8JD for supplying china and props.
Computerset by Chapterhouse, The Cloisters, Formby L37 3PX
Printed and bound in Italy by New Interlitho, S.p.a., Milan

Contents

To my wife and daughters

Thanks to the people who have influenced my life most:

My Mother
Dott. Bepi Santin
Professor Albano Mainardi
of Instituto Alberghiero di Stresa
Peter Glynn-Smith

A special thanks to Anthony Blake, for insisting for so many years that we do this book together, and to Yvonne McFarlane for making it happen. Thanks also to Trisha Mitchell Vargas, Sue Fleming, Guiseppe Roselli, Danilo Minuzzo and all my colleagues in Italy for their collaboration.

Foreword

Food has become the obsession of the Eighties. In our society there are groups of people who concentrate endlessly on the subject, each with a different axe to grind: there is the health lobby with its strict code of what we should and shouldn't be putting into our mouths; those who worry over our methods of food production and the chemicals now added to nearly everything we eat; those who regard food as a new form of status symbol and treat a meal in some restaurants with the reverence normally accorded a concert of classical music or the opening night of a new play. Elevated to the gastronomic equivalent of the movie star, the chefs who produce these works of art have begun forming their own Academies and awarding themselves Oscars. There is another, worthier, group whose prime concern is the growing hunger in the Third World.

Food is my business and my passion, so I am adding my own contribution to the list. Since I am Italian, I want to talk about Italian food, *real* food. It concentrates on freshness, color, texture and taste. A feast for the eye as well as the palate, it is beautiful in itself without also needing to be pretty. It is true to nature and is never distorted into something which it is not. If mushrooms appear in an Italian dish, for instance, they are there for a purpose and you have no doubt that they are mushrooms. They are never transformed into a delicate pinky sauce or an airy mousse. I like to see what I'm eating, to be stimulated by the freshness and appeal of the ingredients, not by the wizardry of the chef. One of the delights of Italian food is that before you is a dish where the ingredients are the stars, each chosen only for its quality, presented simply and at its best.

People who have been to Italy and found for themselves the simple *trattoria* where the food is delicious, the service charming and the bill a pleasant surprise will already be nodding their heads in agreement. But those who have fallen foul of the dismal tourist traps, or who have only tried Italian food in restaurants abroad, will probably have a more cynical opinion on the subject. This, then, is one of my reasons for writing this book: to introduce to those who have never experienced them the real joys of an Italian meal, and to explain why such joys are sometimes hard to find.

My book concentrates on the cooking of the Veneto – because one must begin somewhere and I am after all a Venetian. Accompanied by my friend Anthony Blake, who also happens to be one of the best food photographers in the business, and a retinue consisting of my wife and daughter, Anthony's assistant and an *organizzatrice*, we diligently munched our way through some of the best cooking to be found in Venice and the other towns of the Veneto – all in the line of duty, of course.

Dispelling the myth

I'm tired of hearing that 'in Venice you don't eat well', that the restaurants are bad and the food is dull and heavy. The places I will mention, both in the city and elsewhere, are all capable of providing excellent food. I know because I have been eating in these restaurants for years. I also know that if you go to any of these establishments and say, 'I have been highly recommended to eat here and I would like to try this partic-ular dish', they will be delighted to cook something special for you. Italians are a proud people, but we are not arrogant. If somebody expresses a desire for something different, and doesn't mind waiting a few minutes more for it, we are more than happy to oblige and show you just how good our cooking can be.

For those who would like to try these dishes at home I have included many of my own favorite recipes. These are all based on the traditional cooking of the Veneto, with a few innovations which I have made to make them suitable to the current taste for lighter cooking. Also included are some of the specialities of the restaurants we visited, so that if you should happen to be in the area you will be able to try them for yourself and draw your own conclusions.

I have strong views on Italian food and its reputation abroad. I'm writing this book to put my case for a new appraisal of our best, classic dishes. It is time justice was done, but I don't intend to preach. I'm simply saying, 'Here is beautiful, proper food, this is how it's cooked. Try it.'

Introduction

Having warned you of my strong views on Italian food, perhaps I'd better begin by establishing my credentials. I do know what I'm talking about, I've been involved with food all my life.

I was born in the Hotel Centrale, Jesolo, which, in those days, just before the Second World War, was a quiet little town of some 400 to 500 people. It was very beautiful and completely unspoilt with 18 kilometres of fine yellow beach which in the short summer season attracted the wealthy landowners of the region. The sort of people who now, perhaps, might holiday in the Caribbean would arrive in their carriages – for there was no road link between Jesolo and Venice as there is today – when the season opened on June 24th and stay in one of ten hotels, the Casa Bianca, the Grand or the Centrale being the main ones (the latter owned by my parents). By August 15th, *Ferragosto*, they had all departed and the sleepy little town went about its business again for another year.

Actually, the names of the hotels were somewhat grander than the hotels themselves, for with the exception of the Grand Hotel they were really only an extension of the original *osteria con alloggio* which, like the hostelries in England, had existed for centuries in country towns. My grandparents on both sides of the family were from Jesolo and had been in the *osteria* business, so it was only natural that my father would run a hotel and my mother a notable kitchen. She was an excellent, simple cook, full of ideas and with a real interest in food. My family was able to found a mini-empire around her cooking for, as the business grew, my four older brothers also joined it and, although all trained in other professions, they each maintained an interest in hotel-keeping.

I think it was because I was the youngest that my passion for the business, especially the food side, developed more than in my brothers. Perhaps because I was the last one, my mother tended to have me with her in the kitchen more, taught me more, relied on me more. It was a curious life, I suppose, but I never knew anything else. I ate always in the restaurant or its kitchen; I watched television in the hotel TV room (therefore I could never *choose* my programmes, the guests came first); I always slept in a room with a number on its door – and indeed at the height of the season I would never know in *which* room I would be sleeping that night (often, in fact, I was obliged to sleep in a bathroom!). I lived in hotels throughout my youth, and it wasn't until I went to England that I lived in a *house*.

Apart from the fact that my mother's cooking made our restaurant successful, she also had a sound business sense which brought a singular financial advantage to the family: she applied for a licence to sell salt and tobacco, and, against all the odds, was awarded one. Let me explain: *sale e tabacchi* were the only commodities in Italy with state-controlled prices, and in order to sell them you had to be granted a licence based upon the

16

population figures for the area. The licences are hard enough to get today, but they were almost impossible then. The result of our acquisition of the licence was that everybody in town came to us for their salt and tobacco.

When the war came to Jesolo my family was fortunate. Since the Hotel Centrale was the only establishment still open, whoever happened to be winning at the time stayed with us: we became the headquarters first of the Italian Army, then the Germans, next the Americans and finally the British. I was still a very small boy and was kept out of the way most of the time, but I do remember when the Germans blew up all the marine fortifications and the whole of the *Terra Ferma*, which is built on reclaimed land, became flooded once more. It turned into a paradise; every kind of flora and fauna appeared and there were many new kinds of fish and waterfowl for the pot. I seem to recall that the beach had been mined and that I used to play on it – a singularly foolish thing to do – before the malaria which also flourished in our new environment caught up with me, as it did everybody in town.

In 1946 I was sent away to boarding school. When I returned in the holidays I wasn't told, 'Here is some money, go and amuse yourself,' it was, 'Here is a cloth, go and wash glasses in the bar.' It was around this time, just after the war, that Italy enjoyed its famous 'economic boom' and Jesolo began to grow as a holiday resort. It was at this point that my mother's foresight paid off. We still had the only licence for the sale of salt and tobacco in town, because Jesolo still had a nominal population of 500 or so. During the short summer season, however, this number would swell to 5,000, and all of them queued up to buy their cigarettes and the stamps for their holiday postcards from us. Today there must be twenty or

Overleaf

The Rialto market on The Canal Grande. Deliveries of fruit and vegetables are made daily by boat to the restaurants of Venice.

more *tabaccherie* serving Jesolo, but for the entire duration of the 'boom', while Jesolo was growing, ours was the only one. Next door we wisely installed a bar to keep the queue happy. It had an eight-group coffee machine, a rarity in Italy even today, so we could keep pace with demand. We were serving over a thousand coffees a day and I, who as the smallest had the most important job, would go round at intervals with my broom to sweep up the empty sachets of sugar, unable to see my feet through the sea of paper. At this time, thirty-five years ago, we were taking something like two thousand dollars a day during the holiday season!

People only had a few short weeks to make their money for the entire year, or else they would be forced to live on credit until the tourists returned. During this ten-month 'out of season' period Jesolo mush-roomed, hotels sprang up, existing places were enlarged, and in 1949 our own hotel suddenly grew into one of 90 rooms. Waiters turned into brick-layers, and hoteliers built their new places with their own hands. Fortun-ately nothing ever fell down, but because the growth was entirely un-planned the town started to look decidely odd with new bits added on here and there as people made enough money to expand. The winters were as hard as ever: there was nothing much to do and people had to live in cold, empty buildings intended only for summer use. However, nobody left town as at other resorts because it was during the winter that the real business in Jesolo was done: land would be bought and sold, sometimes changing hands six times over before the tourists returned. Speculation was rife in those days, and fortunes could be made or lost.

Because we ran a restaurant my family was able to profit from the tourist trade in another way: on fine Sunday mornings in early spring people would drive down to Jesolo to book their hotel room or holiday flat for the summer. My brother and I were despatched to stand in the road and persuade visitors to come to us for lunch. It was impossible to estimate in advance if we would do much business because everything depended on the weather – if it was raining everybody would stay at home – so our suppliers were on standby and, having brought in the custom, my brother and I waited at table, virtually running to the fish-monger or the grocer every time we took an order. The kitchen was staffed by local girls who came in on Sundays for low wages, good experience and lunch. My mother was in charge and was ably assisted by my sister-in-law, an excellent, very disciplined and very clean cook. I learnt a great deal from watching them.

Although I had to work so hard I was really inspired to run a restaurant of my own when I grew up, and tried endlessly to convince my brother we should go into business together, but he was four years older than I and determined to be a veterinary surgeon instead. Eventually he became a doctor and we still laugh at my persistence in those days, a determined thirteen-year-old who wouldn't leave him in peace. Nevertheless I was a normal child, not over-obsessed with work, and I remember how I tried to get out of doing my share whenever I could. When we were at our busiest we had to eat lunch in shifts, three brothers sitting at table with my parents while the other two worked out front. Therefore, whichever two boys finished first had to go and relieve their brothers. I made a point of taking my time, eating more and more lunch so that I wouldn't be one of the relief team!

As my schooldays drew to a close a big row brewed between me and my parents. They wanted me to continue my education and go into one of the professions, while I wanted to get into the restaurant business. Eventually my father compromised by setting me to work for the man who made the pastries and cakes for us. I spent a year as a *commis pâtissier*, but I didn't enjoy it much. *Pâtisserie* is a matter of chemistry, and there is very little room for your own ideas because everything is made to a formula – change that and the recipe won't work. No matter how experienced, a *pâtissier* has to measure things out carefully and observe all the rules, and the only scope for imagination is in assembly and decoration. Cooking, however, is a matter of alchemy – of dedication, looking, tasting, understanding and loving – and was much more what I wanted to become involved in.

When I was seventeen I persuaded my parents to let me attend the hotel school in Stresa on Lake Maggiore. It was prohibitively expensive – 100,000 *lire* a month 30 years ago was a considerable amount of money – but it was worth every penny. The course was the toughest thing I've ever done, but I have no doubts at all that it altered my life completely. I was one of 70 eager pupils at Stresa who would be slowly pared down to just 25 at the end of a gruelling three years. We were on trial the whole time, as we could be expelled at any moment for any reason if it was felt we would not make a good hotel manager. And there was no respite during school holidays, for we were packed off to work in hotels, and those reports were also added to our marks.

Despite such a daunting standard I did manage to graduate and was lucky enough to have received the best possible education in hotel management. The hotel school was a new phenomenon then, and was run by former staff of the many first-class hotels in Stresa (long a famous resort) who, thinking of retirement, had turned to teaching. Thus it was that our classes were held by the very best people in the business – the best chefs, waiters, managers and hall porters all passed their knowledge on to us. It was difficult, though, as every step of the way we were assessed, and if found wanting it was expulsion with no grounds for appeal. I remember one poor boy was sent home only three months before the finals. Nevertheless, I enjoyed the course enormously and felt privileged to be learning from such talented and dedicated experts: people who

An early morning boat on the Canal Grande delivering fruit
and vegetables to Venice's restaurants.

spoke several languages and had travelled the world at the top of their profession devoted all their energies to teaching us everything they knew.

After receiving my diploma I returned to Jesolo and took over the running of our hotel. At barely twenty years old, I was still the baby of the family, but I was also the only one with a full professional training. What I lacked in experience I made up for in education as the only 'expert' among my own self-taught people. My family was very proud of me, but naturally there was also some conflict. I was full of new ideas and wanted to make alterations and improvements; my family had run the business for years and didn't necessarily respond well to my innovations. Furthermore I was sixteen years younger than my eldest brother, so it disturbed the pecking order somewhat when everyone ran to me at times of crisis. Our disagreements were minor, however, and we were never really rivals.

As the business grew and we opened more hotels I moved on to running nightclubs in Jesolo, Milan and Cortina. By this time Jesolo had become very popular, the season was much longer, and foreigners as well as Italians began to arrive in ever-increasing numbers. Today Jesolo is the largest holiday resort in Europe with 600 hotels and about 10,000 holiday flats. Nowadays Venetians drive down to sip an *aperitivo* on the seafront before returning home for dinner. They take their holidays farther afield. It was during this nightclub period that I had the good sense to marry a beautiful English girl who was working in Jesolo at the time. As well as two lovely daughters, Maggie has also given me tremendous support in my business, helping me to run my own hotel in Jesolo for six years until the day we decided it was high time we move to England and have a go at running our first proper restaurant.

It was always my dream to open a serious restaurant of my own, and my first venture was in West London. This was a success, but I wanted to move further into the city, and I achieved that ambition when I opened

Santini in Belgravia in October 1984. That, too, was received very well – and still is – and I have recently opened L'Incontro in Chelsea to enthusiastic reviews.

All the dishes I serve reflect the classic ways of cooking in the Veneto. The use of herbs, for example, is very much based on my background and the way I learned to cook. In the South, they use marjoram and oregano. Around Venice we use subtler flavorings – sage, rosemary, basil. We use less chili pepper than they do. In the past, in the North, we may have used a lot of animal fat in cooking and fattier cuts of meat. Nowadays we are getting away from this and using leaner cuts.

The menu at Santini is short. When I first came to London's West End I was aware that there were already a lot of Italian restaurants around. Ours had to be special. I wanted to create a menu that I could have created in Venice. So I put as much emphasis as possible on authentic Italian dishes and it worked from the beginning. Unlike the others, we had very little pasta and veal on our menu. We had risottos and seafood. We were very worried then that other smarter Italian places were opening all around us and that they would imitate what we were doing. But none of them did. Their décor may have been different, but the menus were the same old clichés.

The atmosphere is different in L'Incontro, but the quality of the food is the same as at Santini. We emphasise seafood more at L'Incontro and the piano bar downstairs attracts a slightly different clientele. At Santini we have around six or seven pasta dishes and a similar number each of meat and fish dishes. The emphasis is always on the freshest ingredients chosen according to seasonal availability.

I planned the menus to be short and consist of classic Venetian-style food, which we do well. As we built up our reputation and customers came regularly we developed variations on the classic themes to add

L'Incontro, *opposite* and Santini, *above*,
the author's central London restaurants.

variety – both for the customers and for the brigade in the kitchen. They in turn have become specialities and the menu has grown. Now people come to us from all over the world – we regularly take bookings made from America and Europe. People read about us and come to taste our specialities, the dishes that have made our reputation – Pasta Mista, a selection of pasta, Risotto Primavera, risotto with spring vegetables, Carciofi Santini, braised whole artichokes, Branzino Santini, sea bass with fresh herbs, Anguilla in Umido, braised eels, to name just a few.

I love the business, and consider myself very fortunate because, having been trained as a hotel manager, I was taught how to be a chef, a waiter, a barman, a book-keeper and a *maître d'hôtel*. Anyone who wants to make a success of business should know it from top to bottom. Many restaurateurs have connections, money and enthusiasm but end up at the mercy of the chef: if the chef wants to change the whole menu or demands an enormous pay rise he can effectively blackmail the owner, for without the kitchen there is no restaurant. If ever I was put in such a position, I could say, 'Well, leave. I'll spend the next week in the kitchen preparing lunch and dinner until I replace you.' Good restaurateurs have to be completely involved in their business, in everything from the décor to the side salads, so that they don't feel like a foreign body in their own establishment; so that they can feel sure that what the customer receives is exactly what was planned when the restaurant opened; so that they can sleep at night. With three restaurants, a thriving business that I love, and with Maggie still at my side, I am a happy man.

The cooking of Italy

Firstly it must be said that there is literally no such thing as *Italian* cooking. Until 1861, when all the separate and individual city states were unified, Italy, both politically and geographically, was strictly regional, and so, too, was its cooking. The cooking of Italy, therefore, is as varied as if the country were composed of *many* countries.

The Italians had long had a great love and respect for food: we have much evidence of what and how well the Ancient Romans ate, and from then on Italy was perhaps the most sophisticated country in Europe in a gastronomic sense. For instance, it was the Italian cooks of the Renaissance who were to revolutionize cooking in both Italy and France. In 1553, when Caterina de'Medici travelled from Florence to France to marry the future King Henri II, she was purportedly accompanied by a retinue of chefs and pastry cooks whose influence became widespread in her adopted country. When Maria de'Medici followed in her footsteps some 60 years later, to marry Henri IV, France began to take the lead over her mentor, and indeed chefs from the French court were said to have been sent back to Venice to demonstrate their skills.

There was much criticism at this time of what the French were doing with food – masking it in sauces, transforming it into something unrecognisable – and this could still be a blueprint for the differences between French and Italian food today. Italian food is *real* food, simple food without undue complication, fresh ingredients unspoiled by elaborate cooking methods. Often the dishes are not plain, but still show the food at its best – one must always respect one's materials. There are no soufflés and no terrines, as Italians like simplicity and excellence, disliking food transformed into something else. In a way it seems like cheating – to me anyway – to whizz up in a blender a beautiful *minestrone* – a delicious fresh soup full of different colors with the crunchiness of some vegetables complementing the smoothness of others – to make a bland cream soup of uniform color. This might be something a restaurant or a thrifty home cook would do with a

One morning, very early, I got a lift in a
mototopo delivering fruit and vegetables from the Rialto market
to the Danieli hotel.

minestrone three days old, when it couldn't really be served as *minestrone* any more. Similarly, if you cook half a lamb, you can serve some of it, and with any leftovers you might consider making a terrine. What I don't believe you should do is *start* to make a terrine, any more than you should *start* to make a cream of vegetable soup. And why prepare a mousse of salmon when you have a lovely fresh piece of salmon you can cook in a better way? Because Italy has such a wealth of good ingredients, Italians treat them simply, with loving care – and the cooking is good, wholesome and hearty.

Because of this basic simplicity in approach – cooking in Italy is really good *home* cooking – Italian food has been misunderstood and undervalued when it has been exported. This is mainly due to the fact that most people who leave Italy to open restaurants elsewhere are people who have worked in hotels, and the cooking has therefore been of the hotel variety, an important point to take into consideration when assessing Italian restaurants.

Hotel cooking versus restaurant cooking

Up until about 15 years ago every hotel in Italy, even those in the five-star category, operated on a full or half-board basis. The guests ate in the hotel restaurant once or twice a day and there was no need to attract custom from outside, therefore the chef was chosen not necessarily as the person who could cook best but as the one who could feed a lot of people economically – cutting the steaks a little finer, making second-class vegetables look first rate and so on. With, say, 250 *table d'hôte* guests at every sitting there was no pressure on the chef to be inventive and give of his best; so long as the guests were reasonably happy and there were no serious complaints, the economies could be made.

People in the catering trade who emigrated (there are sizeable populations of Italian immigrants in every European country and all the larger cities in America and Australia) came almost exclusively from the hotel business and brought their former habits with them. Those who had previously worked as hotel chefs, waiters and so on now took jobs with the major hotel chains and worked there long enough to be able to afford to open a restaurant of their own. Thus the majority of Italian restaurants that we know in London or Manchester, New York, San Francisco or Sydney are largely the inspiration of those who have never known a true passion for cooking Italian food in the best possible way.

There has always been these two forms of cooking in Italy, the hotel and the restaurant, and sadly very few *restaurant* proprietors or chefs have ventured into their own businesses abroad. Unlike a hotel, a restaurant has no guaranteed clientele, so if it doesn't give maximum value for money – which means the best-quality ingredients and cooking – customers will not be attracted to it, and will certainly not return. A good restaurant *must* have food as its star attraction, for there is no other reason to visit it or to pay good money (there are much better places to discuss business or to fall in love). The restaurant chef must have that passion, while the hotel chef has no stimulation in his work, repeating the same meals over and over again. The best analogy I can think of is the difference between fashion design and making uniforms: the designer must continually think of new ideas, which people will want to buy and which will enhance his reputation and so ensure his future success. The uniform maker has to repeat himself endlessly with little hope of doing something different tomorrow. He may be good at what he does, but economy and uniformity are his only criteria.

I have a simple rule of thumb which rarely lets me down: no-one can run a good Italian restaurant abroad if they haven't tried running one in Italy. Italians know about their own food and unlike the English are not too 'polite' to make their complaints felt if the food doesn't come up to expectation. Foreigners who don't know what they ought to be offered have generally been fobbed off with that ghastly, pseudo-Italian, 'international' style of food where the demi-glace is king and the béchamel its consort. Béchamel or *salsa balsamella* is in fact an Italian invention, but it is far from universal, and has rather become the province of the French. Demi-glace has no place in Italian cooking what-soever, and if there are two spoonfuls of thick brown sauce on your *scaloppina al Marsala*, then you've not been given the real thing. (Italian food is usually served without a sauce, unless it has been stewed or braised and the cooking process has created a sauce of its own. A sauce may also be served with a very plain dish to give it an extra dimension, and pasta or *gnocchi* naturally require this, but again, béchamel will only be used to moisten such dishes when cooked in the oven.)

The problems of catering for people who have not experienced a particular style of cooking on its home turf are certainly not unique to Italy and to some degree it's natural for immigrants to adapt their food to suit the taste of their customers. Similarly, in a city like Venice, which is inundated with tourists year in, year out, it's likely that standards will slip when a restaurant caters for people who do not know what they *should* be eating, and will eat it anyway, whether it's up to standard or not. Even people who try to do interesting things will become dis-illusioned when the response is merely average, and no different from that received by the banal tourist trap next door. People can't help but feel, 'Why bother?' Even the most dedicated among us need to feel

——— *Overleaf* ———

A display of food at restaurante Da Lino in Solighetto.

appreciated for what we do, and if you know that it will make little difference either way you will inevitably start to lose interest, and what was once a passion will become merely another job.

Naturally, I'm dismayed by the way Italian food is regarded abroad, but it's not necessarily anyone's fault. Nowadays the reputation of our food rests largely on the pizza-pasta outfits which have mushroomed in many major cities of the world. Pizza is nothing more than Italian fast food – we invented it and the Americans copied and expanded the idea. There is nothing wrong with these establishments – indeed I have one myself – but by no stretch of the imagination can they be regarded as Italian restaurants, where care is taken to cook interesting dishes and present them properly. The *trattoria* abroad is seldom any better, a poor substitute for the genuine article, which, in Italy, has always been a simple cheap eating place, invariably a family business, where you could have a quick bite or a full meal. The *trattoria* exported abroad is not what I regard as a proper restaurant.

Italian food does not have the glamour of French cuisine, but perhaps we will arrive at that point before too long. I hope that eventually we will have the same pride in our cooking and be held in the same esteem because I believe we actually have a wider range of dishes to put on the table. Just think of our starters – I don't mean *hors d'oeuvres*, because where the French have pâté, we have salami – but the soups, the *risotti* and the pasta dishes. The French have nothing to compare with those. I'm not saying that Italian food is any more important than French, but it is *as* important. I wouldn't say that either nation had much to teach the other, but we both still have some things to learn. I eat out as much as I can, in all kinds of restaurants. You learn much from eating the food of another country, although I don't try to copy it. It would be easy, for example, to produce a fantastic spaghetti with curry sauce, but that's not what I'm trying to do in my restaurants. In a way perhaps Chinese cooking comes closest to Italian: the Chinese don't invent new dishes, they stick to tradition, but good Chinese restaurants make improvements and innovations and the standard of Chinese cooking abroad has improved tremendously because of them.

There have been more innovations in Italy in the past ten years than in the whole of the century before. I believe it's because the Italians have finally realized that they *do* have as much to say as the French when it comes to food. It's the same with our wines. For many years Chianti, Valpolicella and Frascati were almost the only wines widely available abroad, and the situation wasn't much better in Italy – there you drank Chianti in Florence, Valpolicella in Verona and Frascati in Rome. Now every region is trying harder to market its wines both at home and abroad. In this we are still a long way off from the French – but the gap is swiftly closing.

The cooking of the Veneto

The Veneto, between the base of the Alps and the Adriatic, lies in the only extensive plain in Italy. Known for its dairy produce, it is well irrigated, it has rich soil and a good climate. It should come as no surprise to anyone that I consider the produce there the best in the country!

The gastronomic centre of the Veneto is its capital, Venice. Venetians have always been great innovators, in food as in many other things too. The first fork was used in Venice in the eleventh century; the art of folding table napkins was initiated here; and beautiful glasses

—— *Overleaf* ——

A wonderful restaurant in Treviso is Alla Colonna. Their tables, with sparkling glass, crisp white covers and fresh flowers, are very representative of those in the best restaurants of the Veneto.

37

from which to drink wine were first blown in Murano. The Venetians were also great navigators and explorers, and it was their opening up of the spice trade routes that made Venice rich, and the centre of European fashion and gastronomy in the Middle Ages.

The classic cooking of the Veneto – which is described in more detail in the individual chapters – follows the same principles as those outlined already for the best Italian food. It uses the finest, the freshest, the most seasonal ingredients and cooks them simply and respectfully, adding just a touch here and there that hints at a more exotic legacy (as in the traditional peppery sauce for guinea hen, for instance, see page 152). Seafood (bass, cuttlefish, salt cod, monkfish, eels, shellfish of all kinds), *risotti* and *polenta*, game, wild mushrooms, certain pasta dishes (especially Bigoli in Salsa), dried beans. These are the specialities of the region. Other famous dishes include Fegato alla Veneziana, Fritto Misto, Funghi con Polenta, Grigliata di Pesce. All are included in this book.

The dishes I serve in Santini and L'Incontro, my restaurants in London, are all my own interpretations of the classic cooking of the Veneto. The inspiration for the menu comes from seeing what's fresh at the market, the butcher and the fishmonger. You must center your dish around what's in season, what's at its best right now. Of course now-adays we have everything available all year round, which may be very convenient but also has drawbacks: in Italy, as very little produce is imported from abroad, some things are only available in season there-fore, and restaurateurs can plan an entire menu around such ingredients and thus be assured of good custom. Oh, the pleasure of finding asparagus on the menu again, when you haven't eaten it for so long!

What I've also done to the dishes served in my restaurants, and to the recipes in this book, is lighten them, modernise them slightly, and adapt them to suit the tastes of this health- and figure-conscious age. For our way of cooking has changed quite dramatically in the last 30 or 40 years. This is because our way of life has changed: for the first time the majority of people are dressed warmly, their houses are properly heated, their work is less physically taxing and their work-places are warm in winter and cool in summer. Thus our calorific needs have altered, and we now look for lightness and stimulation in food where once we looked for heat and fuel.

Food has gradually altered to accord with this, and is still in a state of transition – *nouvelle cuisine* made a quantum leap in this direction, providing minimal food with maximum presentation (because you get less to eat you get to admire it more instead) – but I think it has already been superseded by a more natural, but still light and delicate, way of cooking. For example, nobody wants to give up pasta when they visit an Italian restaurant, so my answer is to offer them a little serving of three or four types so they can taste some variety without having to wade through a large portion of just one kind. Again, if people want to eat a more robust pasta dish such as *lasagne* I lighten it by serving not the traditional meat-based sauce but a little *pesto* sauce, which is delicious in its own right and still leaves you with room for something else.

I'm very gratified that a large percentage of my regular clientele are Italians resident in London. They support me in trying to present good, classic cooking without compromise. Of course, I am also still correcting dishes which I've been serving every day for some time: there is no such thing as perfection, one must never accept things and then let the idea go stale. Whenever I introduce a new dish, I try it at home first. I get great pleasure from cooking and eating at home, having lived all my life in hotels – and there are still some dishes which I would like to introduce on my menus but which just don't seem to take off. It may be that you

A busy lunchtime at La Madonna in Venice,
one of the best restaurants in which to try a seafood *risotto*.

have to be born and brought up in Italy to appreciate them, just as a restaurant there may never have any success with something like steak and kidney pudding, no matter how well they prepare it.

If you offered me a choice between eating badly and going hungry I really would prefer not to eat, as there seems no point in eating poor food when it only needs a little more care to make it decent. And if you choose to eat out you ought to be offered something which shows the competence of the kitchen. Maggie and I once went to eat at a very famous restaurant with many Michelin stars, and ordered the speciality of the house. This turned out to be cold breast of chicken poached and sliced, with a little fricassée of tomato on the side. It looked very pretty and tasted fine, but it did not deserve to be the speciality. If I may make

In the kitchens at Da Lini, Solighetto.

another analogy, it's like ice dancing: you get some marks for artistic interpretation but get another set of marks for the compulsory exercises, and the better you perform the more difficult movements, the more you deserve the gold medal. This is how restaurants should be, constantly re-examining their dishes and trying to improve.

As I've often said, I've always had a love affair with food, and as a young man enjoyed scouring the Veneto for places where they cooked the best *risotto* or *pasta e fagioli*. I don't mean expensive restaurants, just places where the food was prepared lovingly and well. I hope in the following pages that I will be introducing you both to food which is prepared thus, and to the pleasures awaiting you in the Veneto, the area where I grew up and developed my passion for life – and for food.

Pasta, Gnocchi and Rice

Pasta, *gnocchi* and rice are served as a first course in Italy – and in the Veneto, of course – and they are on the whole used as a base for other things: sauces for pasta and *gnocchi*, and a variety of fresh ingredients with rice, particularly *risotti*. Often a pasta or rice dish can be served as a light lunch, eaten with a vegetable rather than meat sauce, or they can be the second course of a four-course dinner, coming between the *antipasto* and the *grigliato*.

Pasta

It is popularly thought that Marco Polo introduced pasta ('boiled dough') to Italy – and indeed he is one of Venice's most famous sons – but the Italians, particularly in the south, were eating pasta long before the explorer returned from his famous voyages. Some say that it wasn't until after Garibaldi led 'the one thousand' south in 1860 and Italy became united that pasta was introduced to and became popular in the rice-eating north. Whatever the historical truth, pasta actually didn't become the universally eaten dish of Italy until astonishingly recently, at about the turn of the century.

Generally speaking, the pasta eaten in the north of Italy is of the flat ribbon type – *tagliatelli*, *tagliolini*, *pappardelle* etc – while that of the south is round (*spaghetti*, *macaroni* etc). However, in the Veneto, as now throughout Italy, the regional differentiations are less strict than once they were. After all, it's not the pasta that's really at the heart of

Early stages in the making of pasta –
sheets of dough being prepared before being
cut into *pappardelle*, *tagliolini*, *tagliatelli* . . .

the cooking, it's the sauce, and there are hundreds of variations, some old and some new, and a few of which, in the following pages, are mine. There really is no limit to the ingredients for a pasta sauce – it can be simply the best olive oil and some freshly grated Parmesan, or a vegetable, seafood or meat sauce, all of which will *make* the pasta, which has no basic flavor of its own.

Pasta is really one of the simplest foods – flour and water or flour and egg – and is now considered to make a good contribution to the diet: the carbohydrate content rather than fattening fills the stomach well and for longer (marathon runners eat it the night before a race). The sauce additions can add protein, fat and vitamins but, in our health-conscious society, new sauces must cater to new tastes and contribute fewer calories than the old sauces such as *bolognese*, *matriciana* and *puttanesca*. Those given here are simple, natural and good.

A few initial points. I don't really think much of colored pasta – those 'flavored' with spinach, beet or tomato paste – as the color largely disappears during cooking, and there isn't any real discernible flavor difference. Trying to state an exact time for cooking pasta, too, is a fairly thankless task. It all depends on the type of pasta (whether it's fresh and home-made, or dried), on the size of the pan, on the heat, and on the amount of water. As in all good cooking, you have to *be* there, and then you can take a strand out and taste it for the degree of doneness you like. Spaghetti and other dried pasta can be cooked until *al dente* – with a give to the tooth – but fresh pasta is too soft for that advice to hold true. Instead of watching the clock, you must watch the pot.

Every Italian cookbook has several pages of instructions, and plenty of diagrams, telling you how to make your own pasta. What they omit to say is that it is quite a skill and requires some practice. It shouldn't really be attempted by people who have no experience of pastry or bread making because there is an art to kneading and rolling which takes time to acquire. And honestly, I don't see much point in laboring at home when you can buy good fresh pasta in every large supermarket and a number of specialist shops. Since cutting it properly, even with a cutting machine, is difficult, I would think it's only feasible to make at home if you are using flat sheets for *lasagne* or *tortelloni*. In very few Italian homes do you eat *pasta fresca* nowadays, and indeed in few Italian restaurants.

We do make our own in the restaurants in London, and one of the most popular dishes on my menu is a pasta platter with a taste of a number of house pasta specialities. Here, however, is a fresh pasta recipe for the determined.

PASTA ALL'UOVO

Fresh Egg Pasta

SERVES 4

generous 1½ cups bread flour   3 eggs

Put the flour on to a clean, dry worktop in a mound. Make a well in the center and break the eggs into it, mixing them lightly with your fingers. Begin to work in the flour from all sides of the well with your hands until firm and slightly sticky.

Now begin again, on a clean surface with clean, dry hands, to knead and twist the dough, kneading it with the heel of your hand. Continue kneading and turning it around until it is smooth and elastic and no longer sticky. This should take about 10 minutes.

Pat the dough into a round, flattish shape, dust your worktop, your hands and your rolling pin with flour and begin rolling, rotating the dough after each roll and keeping it in as round a shape as possible. When it is about ⅛ inch thick you must begin to stretch and roll it by running your hands out to the ends of the rolling pin as you go, in order to apply even pressure. Do this a bit at a time, ensuring the dough remains the same thickness throughout. Continue until the whole sheet is paper thin, dusting with flour if it gets sticky. You must complete this part in less than 10 minutes, or the dough will become too stiff. Try to cut and use as soon as possible – or cut and dry for future use.

An ideal way of using fresh home-made pasta is in one of the simplest stuffed pasta – *tortelloni*. There is a variety of delicious fillings. The pasta must be freshly made, and eaten the same day (or frozen).

TORTELLONI

Stuffed Pasta

SERVES 4
1 × fresh egg pasta recipe
filling of choice (see below)

butter
freshly grated Parmesan cheese

Make the pasta dough as described opposite and roll it into a paper-thin sheet. Cut the dough into two equal-sized pieces. Lay one on your worktop and put spoonfuls of a chosen filling in even rows about 2 inches apart. Lay the second sheet neatly over the first, pressing down lightly so that the filling makes a little mound. Cut into even squares, pressing the cut edges together and down firmly.

Cook in boiling salted water – they will be ready about 5 minutes after the water returns to the boil. Check to see if they are done (stuffed pasta takes longer to cook), and transfer to a warm serving dish with a slotted spoon. Add butter and grated Parmesan cheese.

TORTELLONI DI SPINACI E RICOTTA

◆

Spinach and Ricotta

Prepare the filling exactly as for Crespelle con Ricotta on page 80, but blend it into a light mousse before using.

TORTELLONI DI FUNGHI CON RICOTTA
◆
Mushrooms and Ricotta

Prepare and cook wild mushrooms exactly as for Funghi con Polenta on page 104, drain well, and blend into a mousse with an equal amount of Ricotta cheese.

TORTELLONI DI ZUCCA
◆
Pumpkin

Prepare and cook the pumpkin as described in Zuppa di Zucca on page 88. Drain the flesh very well, pressing to get rid of as much liquid as possible, and blend with a little cream, salt, pepper and finely chopped parsley.

If you are adept – or become so – at making pasta yourself, a *tagliolini* dish is another simple one to show off your skills. (Tagliolini are the thinner version of *tagliatelli*, the ribbon pasta of Bologna.) Alternatively, you can use fresh shop-bought *tagliolini*, but don't be tempted to use factory-made pasta or a thicker variety because, especially in the following dish, you will lose the essential freshness and lightness of the tomatoes and basil.

If you can make the tomato sauce for this first recipe from good, fresh San Marzano tomatoes (the long Italian kind, increasingly available elsewhere, see some notes about them on page 87), the true summer flavor will shine through. And don't on any account consider using dried basil, as the pungent flavor of fresh basil is the whole point of the exercise.(Grow some basil plants in pots on a sunny windowsill so that the flavor will be available to you all summer through.)

TAGLIOLINI CON POMODORO E BASILICO

Tagliolini with Tomatoes and Basil

SERVES 2
6 oz fresh *tagliolini*
salt
scant cup tomato sauce (page 87)

5 leaves fresh basil
a large knob of butter
freshly grated Parmesan cheese
 (optional)

Put a large pan of salted water on to boil for the *tagliolini* and, in a separate pan, warm the tomato sauce gently.

Put the *tagliolini* into the boiling water, stirring it quickly with a wooden spoon to prevent sticking. If home-made, it will be cooked in a matter of seconds; if shop-bought, it will take a few moments more, but be prepared for the speed at which it cooks and remove from the heat as soon as it is done.

Meanwhile, tear the basil leaves into small pieces. *Never* cut fresh basil (or arugula) as you will bruise the leaves and ruin the flavor.

Drain the *tagliolini* well, and put in a serving bowl. Add the butter, the warmed tomato sauce and the torn basil and mix well. Serve immediately with a bowl of grated Parmesan for those who wish it. (The rules concerning the use of Parmesan cheese are there to be bent. Many say that you shouldn't sprinkle Parmesan over fish pasta or *risotto*, but it depends on taste: you are cooking to please both yourself and, hopefully, someone else, so don't take away something that might give pleasure.)

TAGLIOLINI CON FUNGHI

◆

Tagliolini with Mushrooms

Funghi porcini (see page 102) would be best for this dish, but you can use any wild *funghi*, girolles or oyster mushrooms.

SERVES 4
$\frac{3}{4}$ lb fresh *tagliolini*
salt and pepper
$\frac{1}{2}$ lb *funghi porcini* or other mushrooms

extra virgin olive oil
2 garlic cloves, halved
finely chopped parsley
butter

Put a large pan of salted water on to boil for the *tagliolini*.

Wash the mushrooms well, then slice and cook them with the oil and garlic as described on page 104. When ready, season with salt, pepper and parsley.

Cook and drain the pasta as usual, add some butter and olive oil, then pour in the mushrooms. Toss well and serve.

The sauce for the following St Mark's pasta – my own recipe – can be further enriched with a little cream if you wish, but this is not a particularly Italian thing to do – cream is not all that popular in Italy.

TAGLIOLINI SAN MARCO
◆
Tagliolini with Shrimp and Mussels

SERVES 2	12 mussels	a dash of white wine
6 oz fresh *tagliolini*	½ onion, diced	extra virgin olive oil
salt	1 garlic clove	cream (optional)
12 shrimp	butter	

Put a large pan of salted water on to boil for the *tagliolini*.

Cook and shell the shrimp and shuck the mussels reserving the cooking liquid from the mussels for your sauce.

Make a *soffritto* of the diced onion and the garlic, frying in a little butter until golden. Add the shrimp and mussels and a dash of white wine, let it bubble for a minute then add some cooking liquid from the mussels and reduce it into a sauce.

Keep this warm while you cook the *tagliolini*.

Drain the pasta, add a large knob of butter and some extra virgin olive oil, then pour the sauce over the top. Serve immediately.

Arugula – or *rucola* – is a pungent cottage-garden herb much used in green salads in Italy. The leaves have an unusually peppery taste when gathered young. This is one of my own recipes. It's very simple and very good.

TAGLIOLINI CON RUCOLA

Tagliolini with Arugula

SERVES 4

¾ lb fresh *tagliolini*

salt and pepper

½ onion, very finely sliced

extra virgin olive oil

½ lb arugula, torn into small bits

a little good stock if necessary

Put a large pan of salted water on to boil for the *tagliolini*.

Soften the onion in a little olive oil, then add the arugula pieces and toss for a moment. Add salt and pepper and, if necessary, a spoonful of stock. Remove from the heat while you cook the pasta.

Drain the pasta, add a little olive oil and then the arugula 'sauce', tossing it in.

Pappardelle are the widest of the flat ribbon pastas – apart from *lasagne* sheets, of course – and are sometimes cut with crimped edges. The sauce here is a puréed version of Carciofi Santini (see page 93), using the artichoke stems discarded in that recipe. It is quite unusual and a very tasty way of using up the entire vegetable.

PAPPARDELLE CON CARCIOFI

Ribbon Pasta with Artichoke Sauce

SERVES 2

6 oz *pappardelle*

salt

4 artichoke stems, washed and trimmed

extra virgin olive oil

½ vegetable bouillon cube

1 sprig parsley, chopped

1 garlic clove, diced

1 cup home-made breadcrumbs

finely grated Parmesan cheese

a little hot vegetable stock (see page 66)

a knob of butter

Put a large pan of salted water on to boil for the *pappardelle*.

Slice the artichoke stems into small rounds. In a heavy-bottomed pan pour a thin layer of olive oil and when just hot cook the artichoke pieces very gently.

Mix the bouillon cube, parsley, garlic, breadcrumbs and ½ cup grated cheese into a powder and sprinkle over the artichokes in the pan. Add 2 ladlefuls of hot stock, allow to sizzle for a moment and then cover the pan with a tight lid. Cook gently for 40 minutes, checking from time to time and adding a little more stock as necessary.

Pass the ingredients through a food mill or put in a blender to make a smooth cream. (At this point you could cool the sauce for later use, reheating it gently with a little more stock.)

Cook the *pappardelle* until *al dente*. Drain and put in a warmed serving bowl, add the butter and pour in the sauce, mixing thoroughly. Serve at once with more grated Parmesan cheese.

A typical *Pasta Mista Santini*.
From top right, clockwise: *penne* with a *Primavera* sauce (page 72); *Pappardelle con Carciofi* (page 53); *Gnocchi con Rape* (page 64); *Tortollini di Spinacie Ricotta* (page 49).

Spaghetti, as I said earlier, is more southern Italian than northern, but I specify it only because it is familiar and easily available. A variety of pasta shapes could be used instead. The following four recipes illustrate most effectively how varied a simple spaghetti dish can be, ranging here from the southern-inspired sauce of eggplant and olives, to the more modern Spaghetti Santini con Langoustine (see page 60).

In this first recipe, it would be normal to incorporate the vegetables into the tomato sauce, but the olives would tend to darken it. As I like tomato sauce to remain a bright, fresh, pinky-red color, I prefer to serve it in the way described, allowing each person to stir the sauce into the pasta for themselves.

W hat could be nicer than a plate of
Spaghetti alle Vongole (page 57) eaten outside
overlooking the Rialto bridge.

SPAGHETTI CON MELANZANE E OLIVE

◆

Spaghetti with Eggplant and Olives

SERVES 4

¾ lb spaghetti

salt

extra virgin olive oil

½ onion, diced

1 medium eggplant

ideally, ⅓ each of red, yellow and green peppers, or ½ red and ½ yellow (do not use too much green pepper as the flavor should be ripe and full)

a handful of good black olives, stoned

2 ladlefuls tomato sauce (see page 87)

Put a large pan of salted water on to boil for the spaghetti.

Heat some olive oil gently in a pan and fry the onion until it is transparent. Meanwhile, dice the eggplant and the peppers and add to the onion in the pan. Cook over medium heat until the eggplant is just *al dente*; don't let it become too soft or it will start to break up. Add the olives and a small pinch of salt.

Cook the spaghetti in the usual manner and warm the tomato sauce gently.

When the spaghetti is cooked, drain it and serve straight on to four warmed plates. Pour a little tomato sauce over each serving and finish with the eggplant, peppers and olives. Serve immediately.

A fresh clam sauce for pasta is very Venetian (as is *any* seafood sauce), although small clams such as those of the Adriatic are not commonly available elsewhere. You could also make this dish with mussels. (See page 113 for how to prepare them.)

Clams do not need quite as much vigorous scrubbing as mussels, but the same general precautions should be taken, discarding any that are open, damaged or giving out any sludge or slime. They also tend to contain more sand than other shellfish, so you should put them through several changes of cold water prior to cooking.

There are two alternatives in this recipe: with tomato sauce or *in bianco*, which is just 'white', with wine.

In either case the cooking method is the same and you can add tomato or not according to your taste and to fit in with the other dishes you are preparing.

Although Spaghetti alle Vongole in Bianco is always served with the clams in their shells, you may prefer to remove the shells if you are cooking the version with tomatoes. In this case, strain the cooking liquor into the tomato sauce and add the shelled clams, bearing in mind that you must start cooking the shellfish a little earlier so that the sauce will be finished at the same time as the spaghetti. It's not really complicated – all the timings are simple to achieve!

SPAGHETTI ALLE VONGOLE

◆

Spaghetti with Fresh Clams

SERVES 4
about 4½ lb fresh clams, the
    smallest you can find
1 lb spaghetti
salt
extra virgin olive oil

2 garlic cloves, finely chopped
a dash of white wine
a little chopped parsley
3 ladlefuls tomato sauce (optional, see
    page 87)

Scrub the clams under running water with a stiff brush and leave to stand for a few minutes in a basin of cold water. Drain, put into fresh water and continue rinsing in this manner until the water in the basin remains clear. Strain and leave to one side while you cook the spaghetti in the usual manner, in boiling salted water until *al dente*.

Just before the spaghetti is cooked, heat some olive oil in a deep pan and gently fry the garlic. When it is just taking on some color add the clams and cover with a lid. Shake vigorously once or twice, add the white wine and continue to cook, covered, for a moment until all the clams have opened. Add the parsley and the tomato sauce if you are using it.

Drain the spaghetti, put it in a serving bowl and pour in the sauce. Mix together thoroughly and serve at once.

SPAGHETTI MARINARA

◆

Seafood Spaghetti

SERVES 2

6 oz fine spaghetti

salt and pepper

8 mussels ⎫

8 clams ⎪

8 shrimp ⎬ cleaned and cooked

1 small squid ⎭

1 onion, finely sliced

1 garlic clove, diced

extra virgin olive oil

finely chopped parsley

$\frac{1}{4}$ cup dry white wine

Put a large pan of salted water on to boil for the spaghetti.

Meanwhile, shell half the mussels, keeping the rest for decoration. Shell the clams and peel the shrimp. Cut the squid into fine rings.

Fry the *soffritto* of onion and garlic in a little olive oil until golden. Add the squid, cook gently for a few moments, then add the rest of the fish, the parsley, some salt and pepper and a good measure of olive oil.

Cook a little longer, while you put the spaghetti into the boiling water. Cook until *al dente*.

Add the wine to the sauce and let it bubble up. Drain the pasta, toss in the sauce and serve at once.

Few pasta dishes are easier to prepare than this recipe following, and in my opinion none taste better. It is a very traditional Venetian recipe which is most often made with wholewheat pasta. You may choose which type of pasta you prefer and if you cannot find *bigoli* you can substitute a thick spaghetti, but you will be lacking one secret element: *bigoli* have a fine hole running through the middle of each strand which cleverly traps a thin stream of the delicious sauce.

BIGOLI IN SALSA

Pasta with Anchovy Sauce

SERVES 4

1 lb bigoli or thick spaghetti

salt

10 small anchovy fillets (canned in olive oil, *not* tomato sauce)

2 large onions, finely sliced

a liberal amount of extra virgin olive oil

a few capers (optional)

black pepper

Cook the pasta in plenty of boiling salted water. Remember that wholewheat pasta takes longer to cook than refined and you must judge when it is *al dente* carefully,

because if anything it's even worse overcooked than the refined variety. It should take a maximum of 5 minutes. Also be careful not to oversalt the water since the anchovies will make the sauce quite highly seasoned.

Meanwhile chop the anchovy fillets and pound them, ideally in a small terracotta pot, into a fine paste. Fry the onion in a little oil over gentle heat until it is transparent. Add the anchovies and cook gently, stirring the mixture well. Pour in a good measure of olive oil and mix the sauce together until it is smooth and well amalgamated. Add the capers if you are using them, then grind in a little black pepper and taste carefully for salt.

Drain the pasta, put in a serving dish – again it looks beautiful in a terracotta pot – and pour in the sauce, mixing it well so that each strand is coated. Serve at once and wait for your guests' compliments. You will not be disappointed!

SPAGHETTI SANTINI CON LANGOUSTINE
◆
Spaghetti with Langoustines

SERVES 2

6 oz spaghetti (use a fine type, like Grade 5)	finely chopped parsley
	10 mussels, cleaned (see page 113)
salt and pepper	10 baby clams, cleaned (see page 57)
6 langoustines (or jumbo shrimp)	$\frac{1}{3}$ cup diced red and green pepper
extra virgin olive oil	a dash of cognac
1 garlic clove, finely chopped	$\frac{1}{2}$ cup white wine
	a knob of butter

Put a large pan of salted water on to boil for the spaghetti.

Split two of the langoustines lengthwise and remove the black intestinal tract; shell the rest (removing intestines similarly), and cut each into several pieces. Put the split langoustines in a small flameproof dish with a little oil and a sprinkling of salt, and place under the broiler. They should be broiled in all for about 3–4 minutes, so time everything else carefully.

Divide the garlic and most of the parsley between two skillets with a little oil in each and fry very gently; do not allow to overcook. Add the langoustine pieces to one pan and the mussels and clams to the other. Cook over medium heat, shaking the pans from time to time to avoid sticking. After a few minutes, add the diced pepper to the langoustine pieces.

Add the cognac to the langoustine pieces and flame for a moment, shaking the pan well. Add one-third of the wine to each pan and pour the rest over the split langoustines, returning them to the broiler.

Add a little salt and pepper to each pan and continue to cook until the shellfish have opened. Take this pan off the heat and remove and discard one half of each shell. Add the shellfish to the langoustine pieces with a little oil and the butter.

Meanwhile cook the spaghetti until quite *al dente*. Drain well and add to the sauce in the pan. Return to the heat and mix well. Serve on a warm plate with a sprinkling of the remaining parsley and the split langoustines arranged on each side.

Gnocchi

Gnocchi – 'dumplings' – was very much a Piedmontese dish at the beginning, but now it is popular throughout Italy. *Gnocchi* can vary enormously in basic ingredient and cooking method: they can be made from potatoes and flour, from pumpkin, from semolina, or *verdi*, from a mixture of spinach and Ricotta cheese; they can be simmered in water then drained and served with butter and Parmesan or a sauce, or they can be baked. Like pasta, they are a second course.

In Venice, *gnocchi* are made from potatoes and are served mostly with a simple tomato or mushroom sauce, some butter and grated Parmesan. In the mountains of the Veneto in Trentino they serve a green *gnocchi* dish called *strangola preti* (strangled priest) – why, I'm not quite sure!

The following is the basic recipe for potato *gnocchi*, a hearty winter dish, to which you can add any sauce you like. Do not attempt to make it with leftover mashed potatoes, they will require too much flour to bind into a dough and as a result will be heavy and dull.

GNOCCHI DI PATATE

◆

Potato *Gnocchi*

SERVES 4

generous 1 lb boiling potatoes (*not* new potatoes)

1 egg, lightly beaten

a good pinch of freshly grated nutmeg

salt and pepper

approx. scant ½ cup all-purpose flour

Scrub the potatoes but do not peel them. Boil in plain water until just cooked. Drain and as soon as they are cool enough to handle, peel and mash.

Add the egg, nutmeg and a little salt and pepper. Stir with a fork and begin to add a little flour. At this point you will find it easier, if messier, to begin mixing in the flour with your hands.

When the dough is smooth but still a little sticky, spread it out on to a floured surface and cut into small squares. Flour your hands well and roll each piece of dough into a *gnoccho*, about ¾ inch in diameter. Flatten each one slightly in the palm of your hand so that it will cook evenly.

Put a large pan of salted water on to boil and when it begins to bubble drop in the *gnocchi*. They will sink to the bottom and then float to the surface. Let them cook a few seconds more then lift out with a slotted spoon and place in a warmed dish.

They are good served with a plain tomato sauce, a knob of butter and a sprinkling of Parmesan, or you can try any simple, robust sauce of your choosing.

Guiseppe and Stefano making *gnocchi* slightly differently in my kitchen at home. Here, in a variation on my technique, they are rolling the dough into a snake, cutting it off in chunks, and forming the shape with a fork.

GNOCCHI CON SUGO DI POLLO IN TECIA

◆

Gnocchi with Chicken Juices

One of the simplest and most delicious sauces for *gnocchi* consists of the juices from Pollo in Tecia (see page 144).

All you have to do is prepare the *gnocchi* while the chicken is cooking, and serve them as a starter before the chicken with the same 'sauce'. Or you can, of course, serve the leftover juices from the chicken served one night for dinner, to use for a simple *gnocchi* lunch the next day. In other words, killing two pigeons with the same shot – or, as the British say, two birds with the same stone!

In fact, any stock or wine juices left over from roasting or braising meat can be used as a sauce for *gnocchi*, the flavors combining well with the basically bland potato taste of the *gnocchi*.

GNOCCHI CON RAPE

◆

Gnocchi with Beets

SERVES 4

1 × *gnocchi* recipe	1 sprig sage
½ onion, finely chopped	2 medium beets, cooked, peeled and
1 garlic clove, finely chopped	cut into dice
1 sprig rosemary leaves	extra virgin olive oil
	a dash of light cream

Put the onion, garlic, herbs and beets into a pan with some olive oil and cook together gently until soft. Allow to cool. Remove the rosemary and the sage, then purée in a blender.

While the *gnocchi* are cooking, heat a little oil in a pan, add the beet purée and the cream, and warm through. As the *gnocchi* rise to the surface use a slotted spoon to transfer them to the sauce, and when all are ready, put a lid on the pan and toss thoroughly so that each *gnoccho* is covered in the beautiful, creamy pink sauce.

GNOCCHI CON POMODORO E CREMA

◆

Gnocchi with Tomato and Cream

SERVES 4
1 × *gnocchi* recipe

$1\frac{1}{4}$ cups home-made tomato sauce (see page 87)
a dash of light cream

While the *gnocchi* are cooking, lighten the tomato sauce with the cream and heat gently through. Toss the cooked *gnocchi* in the sauce and serve at once.

GNOCCHI VERDI CON GORGONZOLA

◆

Spinach *Gnocchi* with Gorgonzola

SERVES 4
1 × *gnocchi* recipe (but see method)
$\frac{1}{4}$ cup cooked spinach

6 oz Gorgonzola cheese
a dash of light cream
freshly ground black pepper

To make the *gnocchi* green (*verdi*), you add some cooked spinach to the basic potato mixture. Cook the spinach in the water clinging to its leaves after washing, and when it is soft, drain it thoroughly – every drop of water must be squeezed out (as for Crespelle con Ricotta on page 80). Chop it finely and mix into the potato mixture, and prepare and cook the *gnocchi* in the normal way.

Meanwhile, melt the Gorgonzola in a bain-marie along with the cream and some pepper, and toss the cooked *gnocchi* in this.

Rice

Although rice is not actually grown in the Veneto, there are more rice dishes here than in any other part of Italy. This must be because of the region's proximity to the valley of the Po river, Europe's most important rice-growing area. Rice was introduced here in the mid-fifteenth century by the Venetians.

There are literally thousands of varieties of rice, but the only one to use for Italian dishes is Italian rice – rounder than long-grain rice, more like pudding rice. Italian rice itself is divided into several categories, but the best to use – and the most commonly available – is the one with large fat grains called *arborio*.

The way any rice cooks depends on the amount of starch in the grain, and the amount of water absorbed, and *arborio* can absorb slowly, ending up soft outside and still *al dente* within. This is exactly what one wants for a *risotto*, Italy's most famous rice dish, and a dish, like pasta, that can be varied infinitely as a first course, with a huge variety of sauces. Rice is also used in soups, and Riso in Brodo and Risi e Bisi are two particular Venetian specialities.

As *brodo* – stock or, more accurately, broth – is an essential element in Italian cooking, I mention it here. It is always used in making *risotti* because it provides both seasoning and flavor; plain water would give you nothing but bland cooked rice. Furthermore, salt is never added to *risotto* when it is cooking, instead your *brodo* should be on the tasty side so that it seasons the rice evenly. Stock is so easy to make at home – and freezes so perfectly – that you need only rely on stock cubes in an emergency. (Good-quality vegetable bouillon cubes and some of the better brands of meat or chicken cubes can be dissolved in boiling water.) If you are making your own stock, though, don't add cubes as well (they're not necessary), and always avoid canned broth, as the taste is too overpowering.

BRODO
◆
Broth or Stock

Brodo can be made from beef, chicken, fish or vegetables as appropriate. In each case you begin with a little carrot, onion and celery and put bones and scraps of meat or fish, or else chopped green vegetables, plus a little salt, into a large pan of *cold* water and bring to a gentle boil, then reduce the heat and simmer very gently, covered, for a couple of hours. Check again for seasoning and, unless you are using it straightaway, allow to cool. If you keep it in the refrigerator you will also be able to chip away the layer of fat that forms on the surface.

You can freeze it easily in ice-cube trays, storing the cubes in batches in plastic bags, so that you have tiny amounts easily available, but always heat it again before adding to any dish you are cooking.

The *brodo* in Riso in Brodo is traditionally derived from cooking Bollito Misto (page 166), and is especially popular in Basso del Piave (at the lower part of the Piave river in the Veneto), where it forms an important part of the luncheon menu at wedding receptions. Weddings there are always considerable events with a minimum of 150 people and consist of three to four days of eating, drinking and dancing (there's usually no time for a honeymoon!).

The first course of the feast is Affetato Misto con Sott'Aceti e Sott' Olio (assorted cold meats with pickled and preserved vegetables), followed by the famous Riso in Brodo, then the Bollito Misto itself. There is then a pause for about an hour to prepare for Arrosto Misto (assorted roast meats), followed in turn by fruit, little cakes and coffee.

RISO IN BRODO

Rice Broth

SERVES 4
6¾ cups good stock
3 handfuls Italian *arborio* rice

livers and giblets of 2 chickens
salt and pepper
freshly chopped parsley

Put the stock on to boil, and add the rice.

Wash the livers and giblets, and cut into thickish slices (if the livers are cut too fine they will disintegrate into the soup). Add these to the *brodo* and when the rice is cooked – after about 15–30 minutes – season with salt, pepper and a little chopped parsley. It's quite a thick soup.

RISO CON TOCCHI

◆

Leftover Rice Soup

Tocchi means little pieces, or leftovers. To the previous Riso in Brodo recipe add 1–2 peeled, diced potatoes, some diced, cooked chicken and, if you like, some finely sliced carrots. I would not recommend adding anything else or your finely flavored soup will become a hotchpotch of leftovers. However, you can vary the basic recipe with any two or three ingredients of your choosing. It is a simple yet delicious soup.

Risi e Bisi is one of the most famous and definitive dishes of Venetian cooking. It was traditionally offered to the Doges on the feast day of St Mark, patron saint of the city. Risi e Bisi should not be thought of as a *risotto*, but as a thick rice soup. You should use fresh young peas, not frozen ones, to capture the authentic taste and texture. In the Veneto, it is a strictly seasonal dish, made and served only when the new spring peas come in from Cavallino and Treporte.

RISI E BISI

Rice and Peas

SERVES 4
1 onion, finely chopped
extra virgin olive oil
butter
2 lb (unshucked weight) fresh young
  peas, shucked

4$\frac{1}{2}$ cups good beef or chicken stock (see
  page 66)
1$\frac{1}{3}$ cups Italian *arborio* rice
finely chopped parsley
salt and pepper
freshly grated Parmesan cheese

Fry the onion gently in a little oil and butter, and when it's transparent, add the shelled peas, stirring them for a moment. Add the stock, stir well, then add the rice and parsley. Cook gently for about 20 minutes, or until the rice is *al dente*, stirring from time to time. Check for salt and add a little pepper to taste. When the soup is ready, stir in a knob of butter and some Parmesan.

Risotto

A good *risotto* is one of the most delicious and versatile dishes you can make. It requires patience, though, and you must be prepared to stand over it for about half an hour with no interruptions whatsoever – you can't leave it while you answer the telephone or prepare any other dishes. You must keep stirring it at all times, adding stock little by little. But when you taste the finished result you will feel it was worthwhile after all.

There are two things to understand about making *risotto*: the first is that it isn't a rice pilaff and the second is that it isn't boiled rice. It's *risotto*, a unique, creamy amalgam of rice and flavorings. Almost anything can be added to the rice – seafood, vegetables, meat, even nettles, as you'll see below – which is why it's as versatile as pasta. Most people in the Veneto would choose to eat a good *risotto* rather than a pasta dish; they would decide which restaurant to eat in *because* of the quality of its *risotto*; and would be prepared to travel *miles* to sample the best. *Risotto* is very much part of the Venetian way of eating.

The method for a basic *risotto* is as follows. Sweat a little diced onion in hot olive oil, allowing it to soften but not to brown. Add 2 handfuls of unwashed rice per person, and one for the pan – Italian *arborio*, no other kind will do – and stir it around in the pan until it is hot and dry. On no account allow it to color. At this stage add 3 ladlefuls of good hot stock – use one appropriate to the flavorings, but it must be really flavorful – and begin stirring thoroughly. The rice will throw off starch and take on the correct creamy *risotto* consistency. You must keep this consistency at all times: the rice must not be allowed to get any drier or it will stick; and if you add too much stock, it will boil. Cook over medium heat – too high and it will burn; too low and the

The basic ingredients for a *Risotto Primavera* (page 72) –
Italian *arborio* rice, a good home-made stock and prepared young vegetables.

stock won't evaporate and it will boil – and continue stirring and adding
2 ladlefuls of stock at a time.

It takes 20 minutes to cook *risotto*, so, as you near the end of your
cooking time, reduce the amount of stock in order that it will be the
right creamy consistency at the end. The rice should be cooked *al dente*,
soft but with a slight bite.

With your guests ready at the table, turn off the heat, add a large
knob of butter, a little chopped parsley and some grated Parmesan
cheese. (There's a tradition in Venice of adding Parmesan to fish *risotti*,
but I think this detracts from its lovely fresh flavor.) Pour a celebratory
glass of wine and sit down to enjoy yourself.

Now you can begin to add different flavorings, once you've

mastered the basic plain *risotto*. Most recipes for mushroom *risotto*, for instance, call for the mushrooms to be cooked in with the rice from the beginning. However, I believe that it works better if you give them a little flavor of their own first.

RISOTTO CON FUNGHI
◆
Mushroom Risotto

SERVES 6

¼ lb fresh *funghi porcini*

extra virgin olive oil

3 garlic cloves, halved

4½ cups hot stock (see page 66)

1 onion, finely chopped

1 lb 2 oz Italian *arborio* rice

a knob of butter

1½ tablespoons finely grated fresh Parmesan cheese

finely chopped parsley

Wash the mushrooms in cold water, drain and slice each one into several pieces.

Heat some of the oil in a pan and fry the garlic, allowing it to brown but not to burn. Remove it at this stage if you like, as it will have given its flavor to the oil. Add the mushrooms and stir for a few moments until they begin to throw off a little of their liquid, add half a ladleful of stock, and leave them to cook for a minute or two.

In a separate pan, sweat the chopped onion in some oil, then add the rice. Stir well, add 3 ladlefuls of hot stock and stir thoroughly. When the rice begins to throw off starch, add the mushrooms and continue stirring and adding stock as outlined in the basic *risotto* recipe (see pages 69–70). When the rice is *al dente*, turn off the heat, stir in the butter, Parmesan and parsley and serve at once.

A Risotto Primavera, very Venetian, but not uniquely so, should contain as many different, fresh tastes (and colors) as possible, so include all the following spring vegetables: fresh peas, green beans, zucchini, carrots and mushrooms.

Some people prefer to cook all the vegetables in with the rice, adding them in batches to prevent overcooking, but I find you get a better result if you cook the vegetables separately and add them at the end. That way you don't have to calculate cooking times and you run no risk of having any vegetables collapse into the *risotto* instead of remaining crisp. The quantities stated in the recipe are approximate.

RISOTTO PRIMAVERA

◆

Risotto with Young Spring Vegetables

SERVES 4

1 carrot, scrubbed	$\frac{3}{4}$ cup fresh shucked peas
a few mushrooms	extra virgin olive oil
2 zucchini, trimmed	$1\frac{2}{3}$ cups Italian *arborio* rice
$\frac{1}{4}$ lb green beans	good home-made stock (see page 66)
1 potato, peeled	a large knob of butter
2 onions	freshly chopped parsley
2 garlic cloves	freshly grated Parmesan cheese

Split the carrot lengthwise and slice across into half-moons. Chop the mushrooms into largish pieces. Cut the zucchini into fairly large matchsticks and cut the beans into pieces if they are large. Slice the potato evenly and dice the onion and garlic.

Cook the beans and zucchini in water or stock in separate pans until they are just done and still quite crunchy, a few minutes.

Fry a *soffritto* of onion and garlic in some oil until transparent, without allowing it to brown. Add the carrot, the peas, the potato and the mushrooms. Stir well, then add the rice, stirring it well to prevent sticking. Add some hot stock and begin stirring and adding stock as outlined in the basic *risotto* recipe on page 69.

When the rice is cooked, add the butter, parsley and Parmesan. Mix well and add the par-cooked beans and zucchini, stirring them into the rice carefully so they don't break. Serve at once.

Ortiche – common or garden nettles – have a delicate flavor, like mild spinach, and are said to be good for your rheumatism (which you got from standing in a damp nettle patch).

RISOTTO DI ORTICHE

Nettle Risotto

SERVES 4
1 lb nettle tops
1 onion, finely sliced
2 garlic cloves

extra virgin olive oil
1⅔ cups Italian *arborio* rice
good home-made stock (see page 66)
butter and freshly grated Parmesan

First, arm yourself with a pair of rubber gloves and a basket, then find a healthy patch of stinging nettles and pinch out only the tender little tops. Wash and drain well.

Fry the onion and whole cloves of garlic in a little olive oil until they become golden. Take out the garlic and add the nettles, tossing them gently. Add the rice and proceed to make the *risotto*. When it's finished, add the butter and Parmesan.

There are endless variations on *risotto*, and it would take another book just to get through them, but some quick suggestions could be:

RISOTTO CON ZUCCHINI

Zucchini Risotto

Wash and trim small zucchini and cut into dice. Add three-quarters to your *soffritto* and the remaining quarter 15 minutes later, when the rice is nearly cooked, so they retain some crunchiness. Plenty of butter and Parmesan.

RISOTTO CON GLI ASPARAGI

Asparagus Risotto

Wash, trim and cook some asparagus – in the *brodo* you are to use in the *risotto*. Slice the stalks and add to the *soffritto*, adding the green tips just before the rice is cooked. Plenty of butter and Parmesan. This is one of the very best *risotti*, I think, especially when made with *asparagine*, the very thin new asparagus. The risotto becomes green and creamy, really tasting of the vegetable.

RISOTTO CON FEGATTINI

◆

Chicken Liver Risotto

Clean some chicken livers and cut into largish dice. Add half to the *soffritto* and the remainder 15 minutes later. Plenty of butter and Parmesan.

RISOTTO CON NERO

◆

Cuttlefish Risotto

Take some small cuttlefish (or 2 medium fish for 4 people) and clean them carefully as described on page 121, reserving the ink in a bowl.

A *Risotto Primavera* (page 72), finished in all its glory, ready to be served with a sprinkling of Parmesan cheese.

Cut the fish into small pieces and add to your *soffritto* of onion and garlic when it has begun to take on some color. Add the ink and reduce slowly for about 30 minutes. Then add the rice, let it absorb all the sauce and color, and proceed to make the *risotto* in the usual way, adding a good *fish* stock little by little. When it is ready add a large knob of butter, salt and pepper and some finely chopped parsley.

To try the best Venetian seafood *risotti* in situ, I would recommend two restaurants in particular – La Madonna near the Ponte Rialto in Venice itself, and the Trattoria da Romano on the island of Burano. La Madonna, perfect for dinner or Sunday lunch, is a typical Venetian restaurant with a reputation of 30 years' standing. Pass by here in mid-morning and you will see everyone, from the owner and his son through

The canal on Burano, an island in the Laguna,
most famous – to food lovers at least –
for the Trattoria da Romano.

all the waiters to the humblest young kitchen-hand, intent upon shelling the shrimp and shellfish which will be displayed in time for lunch. This is the place to go if you want to see large congregations of Venetian gentlemen, minus wives, eating together at large tables and talking at length. They may be bankers, *mafiosi* or the work's outing, but they are all serious about food and eager to try the *risotto di pesce*, which is served at table straight from a big aluminium saucepan.

The islands of Murano, Burano and Torcello must be visited if you are on a trip to Venice. Murano you will probably visit only long enough to watch the glass-blowing, but the other two are worth a day each, planned around lunch. In each case, unless you happen to have an arm and a leg to spare for the taxi fare, you will take the boat from the Fondamente Nuove and wend your way slowly up the lagoon, passing the sombre cemetery island of San Michele on your way. Every time the boat stops you will ask yourself, 'Is this it?', but you'll know when you get to Burano because everyone gets off, and most of them are headed for the same place as you.

You follow the crowd along the main street directly in front of the landing-place, turn left, cross over the wooden bridge and continue down until you reach the *piazza*; a little farther along and there is the Trattoria da Romano, one of the simplest and most delightful eating-places you can ever wish to encounter. It was founded by Romano Barbaro, and is now run by his son Orazio, a large, friendly man, and a very good friend of mine. Look around the big, airy room which is his restaurant and you will see nothing but space and light and a lot of tables carefully separated from one another. Look again and you will see that the paintings which cover the walls have been signed by artists whose names make you gasp. Ask about the flags displayed in the simple glass-fronted case and Orazio or one of his loyal staff will tell you modestly that these are the emblems of the *gondolieri* who won this year's *regatta storico*, one of the most famous events on the Venetian calendar, which ranks along with the *carnivale* and the *Biennale*. 'Oh yes,' they will tell you, 'the *gondolieri* celebrate their victories here each year, in fact they were here only last night to put the new flags on display.'

The only concession to the fame of his restaurant is on Orazio's menu, which lists a few names for you to peruse while awaiting your first course. You will be pleased to note that you are sharing a table, in spirit at least, with Charlie Chaplin, Matisse, Katharine Hepburn, Ezra Pound, the Duke of Edinburgh and Federico Fellini. Observe your fellow diners and you may be able to add a few more names of your own, but nobody gawks and nobody cares. Everybody, from the local *buranese* to the famous actor attending the Venice Film Festival is here to eat Orazio's delicious fish cooked over a wood fire in the small kitchen at the end of the dining room. Stray into this room on some pretext and you will observe that the walls are covered in china plates, some of them dating as far back as the sixteenth century. Stay to watch and you will see a small team produce some of the finest dishes in the Veneto.

I think the Romano seafood *risotto* is the very best I have ever tasted, but I have never been able to work out quite why. Perhaps it *does* include some Parmesan? It's more to do, however, with the fact that, as part of the fish menu, the serving of *risotto* is so *small* in proportion to the flavors and pleasures it gives. Many have tried to play tricks on the management in an attempt to amplify the portion: booking for six people with only three turning up was one ploy – but it didn't work!

The following is *my* version of seafood *risotto*. I avoid using white fish because it disintegrates and makes a mess, but I would suggest you make a good strong fish stock from fish heads and trimmings. You should also use the cooking liquid left from the mussels and clams.

RISOTTO DI PESCE

◆

Seafood Risotto

SERVES 6

1 lb each of clams and mussels, cleaned
(pages 57 and 113)
1 lb squid, cleaned (see page 120)
peeled shrimp (optional)
2 onions, finely sliced
2 garlic cloves

extra virgin olive oil
$2\frac{1}{3}$ cups Italian *arborio* rice
good home-made *fish* stock (page 66)
butter
salt and pepper
finely chopped parsley

Cook the mussels and clams as on pages 114 and 57. Drain, retaining the cooking liquid for your stock, and remove the shells. Cut the squid into fine rings. If they are very small, you can leave the tentacles in one piece, which looks more attractive. You can also include some tiny peeled shrimp.

A sizzling hot platter of *Crespelle con Ricotta* (page 80) – pancakes stuffed with a Ricotta cheese and spinach mixture, and topped with a creamy sauce.

Fry a *soffritto* of onion and garlic in a little oil and add the squid, cooking it gently for a few minutes, then add the rice and make the *risotto*.

Add the rest of the fish just before the end of the cooking time and finish with a large knob of butter, salt and pepper and the parsley.

Crespelle

Pancakes are served as a first course, made as thin as pasta and stuffed like *cannelloni* with a variety of fillings. Some are coated with béchamel and baked, others are simply served as they are.

The following recipe for *crespelle* is enough for eight people as a starter, four people as a main course. The filling used in the first recipe is also very good in *tortelloni* (see page 49).

At the Beccherie, one of the best restaurants in Treviso, towers of *crespelle* await their filling.

CRESPELLE CON RICOTTA

Ricotta Pancakes

MAKES 16 PANCAKES
Crespelle
2 eggs
generous cup milk
about 1 cup all-purpose flour
vegetable oil
Filling
1 lb fresh spinach
$\frac{1}{3}$ cup Ricotta cheese
a little lightly beaten egg
a generous pinch of freshly grated
   nutmeg
$\frac{1}{2}$ cup grated Parmesan cheese

a pinch of fresh chopped mixed herbs
salt and pepper
Béchamel
$1\frac{3}{4}$ cups milk
$\frac{1}{2}$ stick butter
about $\frac{1}{2}$ cup all-purpose flour
a pinch of freshly grated nutmeg
a little salt
To finish
tomato sauce (see page 87)
freshly grated nutmeg
freshly grated Parmesan cheese

To make the pancakes, beat the eggs with the milk and sift in a little flour at a time, whisking until the consistency of light cream. Cover and stand for half an hour.

Pour a little oil in a heavy-bottomed *crêpe* pan (or two or three if you are an experienced pancake-maker), rotating the pan so the oil covers it evenly. Heat the oil carefully so that it is hot but not smoking, then pour in a scant $\frac{1}{2}$ ladleful of batter, turning the pan quickly from side to side so that the batter coats the bottom completely. Cook for a few moments until the *crespella* has set and the underside is a light golden color. Turn the *crespella* over with a spatula and cook the other side for a minute or two, then slide it out on to a work surface.

Continue in this manner, laying the pancakes out on your work surface, slightly overlapping if necessary. Don't stack them one on top of the other as they will stick. If you are making them in advance, however, they can be stacked up once cool and stored in the refrigerator.

To make the filling, wash the spinach and cook it with just the moisture clinging to the leaves. Drain and squeeze as much moisture out as you can. Chop the spinach finely and place with all the other filling ingredients in a mixing bowl. Mix it all together very well with your hands.

Roll small amounts of the filling between your hands into a sausage shape, and place on each pancake. Roll each *crespella* neatly, first from one side and then the other. Lay them out in rows, with the fold underneath, on your work surface.

To make the béchamel, heat the milk until it is just about to boil. In a separate heavy saucepan, melt the butter and add the flour, stirring it well with a wooden spoon. On no account let it brown. Remove from the heat and add the milk a few spoonfuls at a time, stirring constantly. Continue until you have a smooth cream, then continue to cook over low heat. Add the nutmeg and some salt and cook, stirring all the time, until the béchamel has the consistency of thick cream.

To finish off the dish, choose a roasting pan just large enough to hold all the *crespelle* and cover the bottom with a layer of béchamel, then a fine coating of tomato sauce. Arrange the *crespelle* in neat rows and cover completely with the rest of the béchamel. Grate a generous amount of nutmeg over the surface and also a little Parmesan. Bake at about 325–350°F for 15 minutes. Serve hot.

You can use any combination of fish and shellfish for these light and delicate *crespelle*, but best of all would be a mixture of shrimps, clams, scallops and some pieces of white fish such as sole or monkfish.

CRESPELLE CON PESCE
◆
Seafood Pancakes

16 *crespelle* as opposite, kept warm
about 1½ lb fish and shellfish (see
   above)
1 carrot
1½ onions

butter
salt and pepper
a dash of white wine
a little béchamel, made as above, but
   without the nutmeg

Clean and cook the shellfish as appropriate. Cut the white fish into small pieces and poach very gently in water containing the carrot and the half onion.

Heat a little butter in a skillet and fry the remaining onion, finely diced, very lightly. Add the fish, season, and continue to cook very gently.

Pour off the butter from the pan and add the white wine, letting it bubble up for a moment before adding a little béchamel sauce to bind all the ingredients together.

Spoon into the *crespelle*, roll them up quickly and serve immediately.

CHAPTER TWO

Vegetables
and Polenta

One of the most spectacular sights in every Italian town is the vegetable market, with its mounds of seasonal vegetables, colorful, glossy, plump and fragrant. In the Veneto, the farmland is particularly rich and varied, ranging from the prolific and lush silt of the fields near the sea to the fertile plains stretching as far as the Alps in the north. The Veneto also has good farming weather: long, hot and sunny summers enjoyed by everyone, and cold, miserable winters grimly endured by all but the farmers – who take comfort in the good effect the weather is having on their crops.

Vegetables have always been of top quality in Italy, as they are very highly prized, and indeed have been for centuries. It is said that Italy's approach to vegetable cooking influenced the rest of Europe, particularly France, in the sixteenth century. This may be partly due to the enthusiasm with which Italy embraced the new vegetables that arrived in Europe after the discovery of the Americas – potatoes, corn, sweet peppers, navy beans and tomatoes.

Although the seasons mean less and less as products are now available throughout the year from all over the world, to Italians, the produce of the season is still very important. What is fresh and available in the market is what will be bought and cooked, as Italians are rather sceptical about, say, peaches at Christmas. (They might buy them, but it will be more for their curiosity value.) I like very much the discipline of the seasons and seasonal produce, not least because it gives you the feeling of waiting for something, of pleasurable anticipation. For instance, I love the once-a-year treat of *asparagine*, thin, tender asparagus, in April. In the area between Jesolo – my home town – and Venice, these are traditionally eaten with hard-cooked eggs. The *asparagine* are cooked then placed hot on a plate. Warm hard-cooked eggs go on top with a dribble of good olive oil, vinegar, salt and pepper and then – I know it's not very polite – with a fork you mash together the eggs with the asparagus tips. One *aficionado* devoured 50 eggs in one celebratory bout! This dish is particularly associated with 25th April, the day of San Marco, patron saint of Venice. The tradition on that day was to give a rose to your girlfriend and to go on a picnic and eat *asparagine* with eggs! (These *asparagine* are also superlative in a *risotto*, see page 73.)

In the Veneto, many of the best dishes are still strictly seasonal. In spring, you will find the new vegetables appearing in Risotto Primavera (page 72) and Risi e Bisi (page 68), the famous Venetian soup which celebrates the arrival of fresh baby peas. In autumn and winter, the warming staple of *polenta* is at its best served with the bounty of fresh wild mushrooms, and restaurants in the mountains hold elaborate feasts devoted entirely to the wild *funghi* which spring up magically after the first autumn rains. Eating vegetables in season is always one of the greatest treats for me.

In Italy, until fairly recently, vegetables tended to be a little overcooked. Things have improved somewhat in the last few years, but I think one of the reasons was that vegetables as an accompaniment have always been less important than salads. Yet many salads actually consist of cooked vegetables, and a number are served as an *antipasto* – like many of the recipes in the following brief section. Vegetables as an accompaniment are usually served fairly simply, parboiled perhaps then quickly sautéed in olive oil with flavorings such as garlic and parsley; a few are baked with butter and Parmesan cheese. Deep-frying is another favorite method, usually in a batter. Vegetables are also used very much in soups and stock, as sauces for pasta and *gnocchi* (which are, of course, *made* from potatoes), and in *risotti*. Many are pickled, and Sott'Aceti (page 166) are a vital accompaniment to the famous Bollito Misto.

In general, salads are simple, and it is not worth giving recipes for them as they are basically leaves or salad vegetables in season, served with a simple Italian dressing. There *is* only one. It consists of good olive oil with wine vinegar or lemon juice, and salt and pepper. No sugar, no mustard, no other additions (except perhaps a quick flavoring from a halved garlic clove) – and it's not mixed in advance; the individual parts are dribbled or sprinkled over the leaves or vegetables to taste, and then the whole is tossed together.

Arugula is one of the most interesting leaves in Italian salads (with this, you don't *need* any spicy flavoring like mustard), and we have many more varieties of this and other salad leaves at our disposal than the rest of Europe. One of my favorite salads is a mixture of beefsteak tomatoes, fennel, arugula and a little onion, but cucumber, lettuce of all kinds and sweet peppers could all be used individually or in combination. The tastes are fresh, simple, very healthy and very Italian – anything that is good and edible finds its way into a salad.

At the Rialto fruit and vegetable market,
stalls piled high with fresh produce are colorful and enticing.

Although I could have given many more recipes for vegetables, I have
decided to go for originality, for more unusual recipes, which would be
representative of the Veneto and its style of cooking. Almost all are to be
served as an *antipasto*, apart from the tomato sauce, the first recipe given
here.

There are only two rules for making this: the first is not to overheat
the oil and garlic, the second is to use the *right* tomatoes. Home-grown
salad tomatoes will not be successful: they contain too much water, which

will evaporate, leaving you nothing for the sauce; and they lack the rich, full taste of a tomato ripened on the vine in hot sunshine. If you think about it, they are grown artificially, even watered artificially, so it's no wonder they are flavorless and sad. A beefsteak tomato in Italy, however, will be plump and lustrous with 'stretch marks', looking as if it were about to explode with sunshine. One of these could make a tomato sauce for about five people, because it contains so much 'meat'!

Whenever you can, when making fresh tomato sauce, use the long Italian plum tomatoes, San Marzano, which are firm, a rich red color, and full of pulp. If you find them fresh – and they are increasingly available in late summer – it is well worth buying them up in quantity and making a lot of sauce (just multiply the ingredients below), which you can freeze in batches for later use. Otherwise you can make a perfectly good *salsa* using the cans of peeled Italian tomatoes to be found in every supermarket and corner shop.

SALSA DI POMODORO

◆

Tomato Sauce

generous 1 lb fresh or canned
   tomatoes
extra virgin olive oil

2 large garlic cloves, diced
a little salt and black pepper

If using fresh tomatoes, chop them in pieces into a bowl to catch all the juice. If using canned, you can chop them in the same way or put them in a blender.

Pour a layer of olive oil into a deep, heavy-bottomed pan and heat it very, very gently. Fry the garlic slowly, letting it take on some colour but not allowing it to brown too much, then add all the tomatoes and their juices. Add a little salt and pepper and cook uncovered over low heat for an hour until the tomatoes reduce into a thick, fragrant sauce.

If made from fresh tomatoes, you should pass the sauce through a food mill to get rid of the pips and skins. Adjust the seasoning and your sauce is ready to use. It is one of the foundations of Italian cooking (although not used as extensively as some people think). It makes an excellent basic sauce for pasta, and a rich cooking medium when stewing or braising meat and poultry. I use a light, concentrated sauce with few ingredients: you'll note I didn't use onion, carrot, celery or sugar in my tomatoes, but let their own summery taste dominate.

Pumpkins, like tomatoes, came from the Americas, and they now grow prolifically in the Veneto. In some parts the flesh is made into a kind of *polenta* – they're also used in *gnocchi* – but a favorite of mine is this soup, interesting to make now that it is possible to buy cut pieces of pumpkin as well as the whole thing (and not just at Hallowe'en). The proportions will depend on the size of the piece you find, but you should use equal quantities of pumpkin pulp and stock.

ZUPPA DI ZUCCA
◆
Pumpkin Soup

SERVES 6
2 lb pumpkin
extra virgin olive oil
2 onions, sliced

1 bay leaf
$4\frac{1}{2}$ cups good beef or chicken stock (see
    page 66)
salt and pepper
cream (optional)

Cut the pumpkin into chunks, removing the seeds as you go. Put in a dish in a very slow oven – about 275° – and cook for about 30 minutes. It will have browned on the top and a lot of water will run out. Drain this off and remove the skin from the flesh.

Heat some olive oil in a soup pot and gently fry the sliced onion and the bay leaf together until the onion has just softened. Add the pumpkin pulp and the stock and simmer for half an hour.

Add salt and pepper to taste and serve as a simple rustic soup, or blend with a little cream for a more sophisticated dish.

The marbled Borlotti beans needed for the following two recipes come fresh in Italy in season (when they can be frozen – very practical); elsewhere they can only be found dried and canned. In fact dried Borlotti are the beans to use for Pasta e Fagioli, which is very traditional and, I believe, the queen of Venetian soups. Made from winter staples, it is heartwarming and tasty, and a strong reminder of my childhood, when I came home chilled to a hot reviving bowl made by my mother.

The recipes can be made using other varieties of dried brown beans, but they will have a different character, and will not be Venetian.

The dried beans used should be bought from a reliable source so you know they have not been kept for too long. If you don't have a hambone – but this gives the best flavor, as it does for the yellow split pea soup in England and Sweden (the Veneto has a similar one) – use some fresh pork meat or a few ribs. In the Veneto they also use some of the extremities of the pig such as the ear to give some flavor and meaty substance to the soup. Do take time over this dish and don't improvise: there are some who would include *potato* to hurry it along to the correct consistency – thick enough for a spoon to stand up in!

PASTA E FAGIOLI

Pasta and Bean Soup

SERVES 5

1 cup dried Borlotti beans, soaked
  overnight in cold water
1 onion, diced
2 garlic cloves, halved
a little chopped parsley
a small piece of celery, chopped
extra virgin olive oil
1 hambone or some fresh pork
salt and pepper
1¼ cups short, tubular pasta
freshly grated Parmesan cheese

Make a *soffritto* of the onion, garlic, parsley and celery, and cook until transparent in a little olive oil in a large pot. Drain the beans and add them to the *soffritto* and fry, stirring well, for a moment.

Fill the pot with fresh cold water, add the hambone or pork, and cook gently for 4–5 hours, stirring occasionally and adding fresh water if need be. Towards the end, add a cup of olive oil.

When the beans are cooked remove one-third and set aside. Pass the remainder of the soup through a food mill, picking meat off the bones and including it (discard the bones). Return to the pot with the whole beans. Check for seasoning, and add some salt and pepper and the pasta. Simmer for about 5 minutes (or longer, the pasta doesn't have to be *al dente*), then turn off the heat and let the soup stand for 10 minutes. Serve with a few drops of extra virgin olive oil poured over each bowlful and grated Parmesan on the side.

If you want to use the dried beans in the following *antipasto* recipe, proceed as for Pasta e Fagioli, soaking overnight and cooking the beans slowly. However, there really is no need to go to this trouble, as the canned Borlotti – particularly if you choose a good brand – are perfectly suitable.

The dish is called *all'uccelletto*, 'little birds', because the same flavorings are used when cooking small game birds. It is very easy to make and has a beautiful flavor.

FAGIOLI ALL'UCCELLETTO
◆
Baked Beans

SERVES 2

1 × 6 oz can or 1½ cups cooked Borlotti
  beans
extra virgin olive oil
6 bacon rashers, cut into small pieces

2 garlic cloves, halved
4 fresh sage leaves
2 rosemary sprigs
a little stock if necessary (see page 66)

Drain the beans well. Heat some oil in a deep pan and fry the bacon pieces. When they have begun to sizzle, add the garlic. As soon as this takes on a little color, add the beans and herbs. Cook slowly, stirring to amalgamate the flavors, adding a little stock if the mixture looks too thick. Serve piping hot. It's good cold, too.

Zucchini as both the Italians and Americans call them – are a popular vegetable in Italy, principally because they are so easy to grow. They are eaten very young and small, very fresh and crisp, and can be deep-fried in batter, fried with garlic and tomatoes, or stuffed if they're larger. The flowers are a very seasonal thing and rarely found as they're so fragile – they only remain fresh for a few hours – but they, too, are commonly deep-fried in a batter (as are marrow flowers in Padua). In the Veneto, the flowers are eaten at home more often as dessert, cooked and dusted with sugar like a doughnut. This stuffed version is my own, and makes a special treat as an *antipasto*. It has the fresh green taste of early summer.

FIORI DI ZUCCHINI RIPIENI

◆

Stuffed Zucchini Flowers

PER PERSON
5 baby zucchini, with flowers attached
½ cup finely diced Mozzarella cheese
a pinch each of finely chopped parsley
   and garlic

all-purpose flour
a little egg wash, made from 1 egg
   lightly beaten with some cream, salt
   and finely chopped parsley
vegetable oil for frying

Trim the zucchini to about $2\frac{3}{4}$ inch from the flower head, wipe with a damp cloth and gently separate the petals to make sure the flowers are quite clean inside.

Mix the Mozzarella dice with the garlic and parsley and put a spoonful or so inside each flower head, twisting the petals to close it again.

Roll the zucchini in flour, lightly shake off the excess, and dip in the egg wash. Do not worry that it doesn't coat the zucchini completely.

Heat the oil in a skillet and quickly sauté the zucchini, just long enough for the egg to brown. Serve immediately. The zucchini will still be firm and the cheese will have melted deliciously into the flower.

Globe artichokes, too, are very popular in Italy and grow particularly well in the Veneto, revelling in the rich salty earth and the warmth of the sun. Larger artichokes can be simply boiled as an *antipasto* and served hot or cold with a dressing, or they can be stuffed – or indeed braised, as in the following recipe.

In the Veneto we can also get tiny artichokes, which can be eaten whole, in salads, with a vinaigrette dressing, in *risotti* or as a sauce for pasta. Known as *castrati*, these tiny artichokes are cut from the main stem to allow the principal head or heads of the plant to develop without interference from a multitude of 'babies'.

These braised artichokes, another *antipasto*, take quite a long time to cook and you cannot stray too far from the stove. Therefore you may decide to prepare them in advance and reheat them later in the day: if doing so, allow the artichokes to cool in the pan, then add a little more stock and reheat them gently. Since the discarded stems are cooked in exactly the same way and used in Pappardelle con Carciofi (see page 53) you might consider keeping two pans on the go and saving the sauce for the pasta for another time.

CARCIOFI SANTINI
◆
Braised Artichokes

PER PERSON
1 globe artichoke
½ vegetable bouillon cube
a little chopped parsley
a little finely diced garlic

½ cup home-made breadcrumbs
1½ tablespoons finely grated Parmesan
   cheese
extra virgin olive oil
vegetable stock (see page 66)

Cut the entire stem from the artichoke (and if you wish, retain for use as above). Trim the top off the central cone and snap off the tough outer leaves around the outside.

Mix the bouillon cube, parsley, garlic, breadcrumbs and cheese into a powder and press this as far in among the leaves of the artichoke as you can. If the leaves are very tightly packed you can heap the mixture on the top.

Choose a heavy-bottomed pan which will hold all the artichokes you are preparing and pour in a layer of olive oil. When this is hot, but not too hot, put in the artichokes and cook them over gentle heat for a moment, then add a ladleful of hot stock and let it sizzle. The artichokes will begin to brown around the base, but this is not important, and will add to the flavor. Cook the artichokes over low heat, covered, for an hour. Check them from time to time and add another ladleful of stock as necessary. Serve the artichokes hot, pouring the pan juices over them.

F*iori di Zucchini Ripieni* – stuffed zucchini flowers
(page 92) – are one of the specialities at Santini.

A dish of *Carciofi Santini* – braised artichokes (page 93) –
ready to begin their gentle simmering in stock.

If it's true to say you haven't travelled until you've seen Venice, it must be equally true to say you haven't really seen La Serenissima until you've been to the *Terra Ferma*, to the Veneto, the heartland which gives Venice its strength and its lifeblood. An ideal visit would combine Venice with Treviso, a charming walled city which is steeped in its own traditions. It's quite easy to hire a car from the Piazzale Roma and drive up to Treviso in less than an hour.

Food is another reason for visiting Treviso. The best radicchio in the world – and most radicchio comes from the Veneto – is from Treviso. Radicchio is the red-leafed, white-ribbed salad plant with a slightly bitter taste (it is a member of the chicory family). Radicchio are winter vegetables, cultivated under straw; as they grow through the straw and snow they look like red snowdrops. The Treviso variety looks like a small red romaine, and has a uniquely bitter flavor. These are unavailable outside Italy as yet, but as we have all been introduced to so many new products in the last few years, the Treviso radicchio will undoubtedly find its way abroad soon. The radicchio which has become familiar recently – the rounder, dark variety like a small cabbage or lettuce – is known in the Veneto as *chioggiota* – from Chioggia – and is not suitable for the following recipe. The consistency is quite different, as the leaves are softer, more like lettuce leaves than the sturdier vegetable leaves of the Treviso variety.

RADICCHIO ALLA GRIGLIA

◆

Broiled Radicchio

For each serving, take a large radicchio and wash the stalk well, checking among the leaves to make sure no dirt is left. Cut it in half lengthwise – or in quarters if the radicchio is very large – and marinate in a mixture of extra virgin olive oil, salt and pepper for a minute or two. Cook briefly under a slow broiler, just until the leaves have softened and begun to color a little. Serve at once as an *antipasto* or as a slimming, sustaining and delicious main-course accompaniment to a broiled fillet steak.

Apart from radicchio, one of the strongest traditions of Treviso is the behaviour of its menfolk, surely a caution to all women who complain of being taken for granted. Around midday the *trevigiano* will announce that he's in need of a little fresh air and will make his way to the Piazza dei Signori, the main square. There he will bump into all his cronies, who also happen to be taking a short stroll. Everyone will celebrate this coincidence with a glass or three of Prosecco, the local white sparkling wine, and some slices of salami, which sharpen the appetite so, 'Why not?', they will all go and have a restaurant lunch nearby. Afterwards they will move on to Alfredo's, Treviso's most famous restaurant, where an upstairs room is specially kept for them to play cards. The afternoon will fly by and it's time for some more fresh air, some more glasses of Prosecco and *pian piano*! it's time for dinner – so off they all go to another restaurant. Diligent husbands may occasionally telephone their wives to let them know about this, but not all do.

It should not be forgotten that *trevigiani* are also astute businessmen: the many shops in Treviso selling elegant clothes, furs and leather are proof of this, and the Benetton empire is a good example of a *trevigiano* family business. All the members of the *giro* are owners or directors of large companies and will nip back to the office from time to time to do a little business, clinch the odd deal and so on. And all the time they are laughing and joking together, their business antennae are waggling away and they miss nothing.

Whether or not you try and give a wide berth to this merry band, you have to visit Alfredo's when you go to Treviso. It's a beautiful

The radicchio of Treviso are quite different in shape and flavor to those commonly available abroad and are easier to broil.

restaurant decorated in the style the Italians call 'Liberty'. There are murals, paintings and Erté numerals to look at, a comfortable bar and excellent food. Alfredo Beltrame was a brilliant restaurateur and a dear friend. Alas, he's gone now, but the empire he founded – the El Toulá chain of restaurants – is growing all the time and has spread as far as Tokyo, and here where it all started you can still feel his presence, as if he's still watching over everything to make sure it's exactly right. It is.

Polenta

Since the discovery of the maize plant in America, *polenta* has been a staple of northern Italian cooking, particularly in the Veneto area. In late summer and early autumn the flat plain of the *Terra Ferma* is turned

To make *polenta*, you sprinkle the polenta flour gradually into the simmering salt water. It is traditionally made in a copper pan.

golden by gently rippling fields of *mais*. This is then ground into flour or meal to be made into *polenta*, and there are various types in the Veneto: both coarse and fine-grained yellow corn meal, and a very finely ground flour made only from the white grains in an ear of corn. This last produces a pale, stiff, almost translucent *polenta* much favored by restaurants in Venice, where they serve it sliced and broiled with a variety of fish dishes.

By tradition *polenta* was made daily in a copper kettle on an open hearth. Today it is made in a heavy saucepan on a modern stove. But while losing some of its folkloric charm *polenta* has lost none of its versatility and soothing nature. It can be eaten as soon as it's cooked, with stews, roasted meat, game or poultry, or it can be left to cool and set, cut into slices and warmed under the broiler or fried in a little butter to accompany fish and grilled meats.

Polenta is an enormously important part of *la cucina Veneziana* and much has been written about the best way of cooking it. Shortcuts have been suggested and additions recommended – some people, for instance, say you should add milk, butter or cream to make it richer, or potato to make it lighter, but I disagree. *Polenta* should be kept simple. It needs no embellishments because it is always served with other things and, if properly made, is quite rich enough on its own.

In the Veneto we say a well-made *polenta* is *come la seta*, like silk, and this 'silk finish' is only achieved by time and dedication. Now that people are busier with less time to spend cooking there may not be someone around ready and willing to stand over a pot of *polenta*, stirring ceaselessly for the minimum of 20 minutes needed to achieve *la seta*. The Italians have turned, therefore, to a mechanical *polenta* pot with an electric stirrer incorporated – an electric *mamma* if you like!

Real *polenta* is made as follows. Salted water is heated in a deep copper pan and when a steady simmer is reached the fine *polenta* flour is sprinkled a little at a time into the water while stirring all the while. When this has been absorbed a little more flour is added, still stirring, and then a little more – exactly as if you were making mayonnaise. Enough *polenta* flour has been used when the mixture takes on the consistency of a rather thick cream soup. The proportions would be approximately $5\frac{1}{2}$ cups water to $1\frac{3}{4}$ cups flour, but naturally the cook must be the final judge.

With the heat still on a steady simmer the mixture is now stirred until the *polenta* swells and the water evaporates – the *polenta* will tear away from the sides of the pan. If it is not stirred thoroughly and end-lessly throughout the cooking time, the *polenta* will not achieve a rich smoothness but will be full of unpleasant little granules.

When it is ready the *polenta* is poured on to a big wooden board – occasionally straight on to a wooden table, or a cloth – and allowed to set for a moment. If it's to be served like this – soft – it is cut with a cheese wire or the string attached to many of the special *polenta* boards. (In the Veneto we joke that a person is so stupid they will starve to death if they can't find the wire to cut their *polenta* with!)

Polenta is an accompaniment to main courses – think of it as a substitute for bread – and in the chapters on fish and seafood and meat, poultry and game, I have suggested many dishes with which the various types of *polenta* go well. One of my favourite, if slightly primitive, treats is to pick up a piece of *polenta* and eat it with a piece of cooked fish on top. It's very tasty. Otherwise I like broiled *polenta* with fish, and soft *polenta*, straight from the pan, with casseroles to mop up the juices.

Another interesting detail concerning *polenta* is that Italians won't eat bread with it. Italians eat a great deal of bread, before the meal, during the main course (even with pasta!), but never with *polenta*.

Since it is hard to find the different flours outside Italy, below is a foolproof recipe for making straightforward coarse-grained, yellow *polenta*.

POLENTA

Polenta

SERVES 4

5½ cups water

salt

1¾ cups coarse-grained corn meal

Pour the water into a large heavy pan, add some salt, and bring it to the boil. Reduce the heat so the water is just simmering, and pour the corn meal through your fingers in a very slow, steady stream, stirring all the while with a wooden spoon as described above.

When all the corn meal has been added, continue stirring thoroughly for a minimum of 30 minutes. When the mixture stiffens and leaves the sides of the pan, the *polenta* is ready.

Pour it on to a clean wooden board in the Venetian manner and serve at once, or leave to harden and cool.

One of the best ways of serving *polenta*, I think, is with *funghi porcini*. Of Italy's many wild mushrooms, *porcini* are the most prized, with a flavor and aroma unmatched by any other. *Boletus edulis* (known as ceps in France) grow in many parts of Europe including Britain, but here they tend to be left undisturbed by everybody except a few mushroom fanatics (usually Italians or Poles, I might add). They can, however, be found in specialist shops, as they are in America and, although horribly expensive, are really worth the investment. Buy as many as you can afford, as they freeze very well and can be used straight from the freezer without being thawed first. Even while still resembling lumpy brown ice cubes their perfume will make you instantly hungry.

I am not fond of the dried *porcini* you can buy in packets. I find the

One of the best ways of serving *polenta*
(here it has been fried) is with gently sautéed wild mushrooms.

flavor harsh and unsubtle, even after the endless rinsing needed to remove all the grit. Cultivated mushrooms are no better; the texture may be an improvement on their dried cousins but the taste is a great disappointment once you are familiar with the real thing.

If the summer has been wet, they'll begin to appear in late August and go on until December. A good, damp autumn will fill the woods with these edible treasures, and many families spend their weekends on all fours with a basket at their side. Indeed, Italians are so fond of mushroom-gathering that in most towns you will find an official expert who will examine your haul and tell you which will be delicious for your dinner and which will lay you flat on your back.

For those who prefer the easier form of mushroom-gathering, Treviso is the place. Every day the mushroom market is held in the Piazza Monte di Pietà, where a handful of venerable old ladies preside over several *bancarelle* piled with *funghi*, usually *porcini*, and the delicate *chiodini* ('little nails'). The ladies keep up a constant chatter, commenting on everybody who passes by and occasionally barking out '*Belli, belli chiodini*' in well-practised voices. Bundled up against the cold, they fortify themselves regularly with a little glass of something from the bar.

These *porcini* are delicious with *polenta* – soft, broiled or fried – to mop up their wonderful garlicky juices. They are obviously best eaten fresh if you're using them for making a sauce, but if you want to preserve them for later on, you can freeze them as they are. For use in salads or as *antipasto*, you blanch them in vinegar, drain them and cover them with olive oil. Season with bay leaf, peppercorns and a little chili pepper.

FUNGHI CON POLENTA

Wild Mushrooms with *Polenta*

SERVES 4
1 × *polenta* recipe
½ lb *funghi porcini*
extra virgin olive oil

2 garlic cloves, halved
salt and pepper
finely chopped parsley

Wash the mushrooms well in cold water, scraping the caps with the blade of a knife. Drain them and cut into thick slices.

Heat some olive oil and gently fry the garlic until it begins to color. Add the mushrooms and cook slowly, stirring them from time to time.

When the mushrooms are soft and juicy remove the garlic, and season with salt, pepper and parsley. Serve at once with the cooked *polenta*.

These cooked mushrooms are very good as a filling for *tortelloni* when mixed with an equal amount of Ricotta cheese (see page 50). They're also delicious with *risotto* and other pasta (see page 71 and 51).

One of the best places to sample wild mushrooms is Al Posta da Lino in Solighetto, run by my old friend Lino. We've known each other thirty years and I used to eat Sunday lunch in the little restaurant he had in the *piazza* at Pieve di Soligo. Now he has an enormous restaurant and is very, very successful. While still in his little restaurant in the *piazza*, he was discovered by Toti del Monte, a famous Italian opera singer who virtually became his fairy godmother. His new place is a collection of cottages knocked into one, so there are lots of little rooms to eat in. There are no walls to be seen because they are all covered in paintings, no ceiling either because that's hung with copper pans. In the autumn one fireplace is stacked top to bottom with little birds turning on spits, and another holds a couple of geese roasting gently.

Like many other restaurants in the Veneto, Lino's has an inner sanctum which you try for, near the big fire and where you are able to see into the kitchens, where his *signora* is always hard at work. She's the last person you see at night and the first one you see in the morning, already making today's pasta while you are hardly yet awake. For Lino has wisely built some bedrooms next to his restaurant so visitors can stay overnight and observe all the bustle next morning as the staff get ready for lunch, and also take the time to look at all the paintings and the little dining room entirely devoted to memorabilia of Toti del Monte. If you need some exercise to give you an appetite, Solighetto nestles at the foot of the mountains. Don't go too far, though, because you must be back at Lino's for lunch!

During the season, Lino serves mushrooms with everything except dessert. He might start you off with some *soppressa* (salami) with mushrooms, then some *funghi còn polenta*, followed by some mushroom *risotto*, mushroom *tagliolini* or mushroom soup; the main course might be *scallopine* with mushrooms. He cooks many varieties in many different ways, and a visit to Solighetto is a must for the mushroom lover.

A few miles down the road from Lino's is a new restaurant opened by Gigetto, who used to work for Lino. Da Gigetto has the same rustic charm, open fires and copper pans and is also very busy. You can eat the same country food as at Lino's: goose, game, *polenta* and mushrooms, and very good it is too.

The white truffle is found in season in every
Venetian restaurant. It keeps best in
uncooked rice.

The wonderful mushroom market at Treviso,
with *una vecchia signora*
selling the harvest of the day.

CHAPTER THREE

Fish and Shellfish

Good cooking always reflects its place of origin, and the Adriatic of the Veneto gives fish and seafood unsurpassed throughout the whole of the Mediterranean in its taste and quality. *Schie, gamberetti, gamberoni, seppie, calamaretti, moleche, granceole, cappe sante, cozze, vongole, anguille, branzino, triglie, sardine, alici, sogliola, coda di rospo* and *baccalà* – I have hardly begun to list the seafood to be found in Venice. They are, respectively: tiny, tiny shrimp, sweet and full of the flavor of the sea; bigger shrimp, no less delicious; jumbo shrimp; cuttlefish; squid; soft-shelled crabs eaten whole (sweet, plump and slightly crunchy); spider crabs; scallops; mussels; baby clams; eel; sea bass; red mullet; sardines; anchovies; sole; monkfish; and, finally, salt cod – a Venetian staple prepared in almost as many ways as there are fish in the Laguna.

Every restaurant in Venice has its display of fish and shellfish nestling on a bed of chipped ice, and decorated with lemons and lettuce leaves. In some establishments you will also see an angry lobster or two with sturdy rubber bands around its claws – a prudent move suggested, no doubt, by an unlucky waiter. If you are keen to eat fish – and Venice is one of the best places in the world to do so – you should always begin by looking to see what's available and what appeals to you. Often the food on display bears little relation to the printed menu, which in many cases is only there for the benefit of tourists who, Venetians believe helpfully, will *want* Spaghetti alla Bolognese or Pollo alla Romana (these and many other well-known dishes are best tried in their place of origin). It's always advisable, too, to try to speak to the owner or manager, to ask his advice about what you should eat. By the very nature of his job, he is passionate about food; it will benefit *you*, as well as give *him* enormous pleasure to see that some of his customers can be equally enthusiastic. This advice should apply to *all* restaurants, but is particularly relevant in a city like Venice, which caters for so many tourists.

If you are truly passionate about fish then you should try to arrange a visit to Chioggia, one of Italy's largest fishing ports and fish markets. Situated south of Venice, Chioggia is very beautiful, like a little Venice in itself. Before dawn the fishing boats are anchored, the stalls set up, and the day's catch arranged in all its glory, a slippery, slithering mass of quicksilver interspersed by the pink and brown, grey and blue 'designer colors' of the shellfish. The market is packed with several hundred brawny Venetians bargaining not at the tops of their voices but behind their hands, *sotto voce*. Prices and deals are a secret! The ground is precariously wet and the air is cold, coffee and *grappa* circulate endlessly, the bargaining is fast and furious, and the fish are unloaded, sold and sent on

The fish market in the Rialto, with a selection of
most of the fish caught in the Adriatic.

their way at a cracking pace – by boat into Venice and through the canals, a wonderful sight for the fish lover.

If your travels should take you into the Veneto countryside, you will still not want for fish. Chioggia supplies all the shops and markets in the region and every large restaurant has one or two days a week which are entirely devoted to fish. This is a fairly recent phenomenon. Until about 15 or 20 years ago, Italians did not eat very much fish, except when they travelled to the coast. Even in Milan, which has a fish market, the quantity was limited and the quality dubious. Now, however, there are more fish restaurants there than in Venice! Even my friend Lino, who runs a restaurant in Solighetto (its speciality is mushrooms), devotes each Thursday to fish. These fish *festas* attract large crowds, who come for a long evening of eating, drinking and talking. The waiters speed back and forth among the tables, the plates of empty shells are stacked high, fingers are licked with gusto as yet more wine is ordered. . . .

There are many wines of the Veneto which are good to drink with fish (see pages 177–181 for more details), but my preference would always be for white. It's up to you, of course, and you might enjoy a light red, a Bardolino, for instance, but I would go more for a local Prosecco, which is slightly sparkling.

There are three ways to reach Venice: the local will drive in, park the car in the grim concrete sprawl of Piazzale Roma and nonchalently climb aboard the *vaporetto* with all the other commuters. The true Venetiaphile will arrive by train, planning to cross the *ponte*, which connects the real world to fairyland at dusk, when the sky is pink and lilac and the air resounds with church bells and the hum of *motoscafi*. First-time visitors should always plan to fly in and take a water-taxi from the airport. As you swing out into the lagoon, you pass half-submerged fishermen collecting mussels from wooden posts, a foretaste of the culinary pleasures to come. This always reminds me of seafood collecting expeditions when I was a boy. In the spring, when the days were becoming more mild, and the tide was low, a few friends and I would plunge barefoot through the water to collect clams. The razorshells were particularly difficult to persuade away from their anchorages, and sometimes the fleshy parts would remain obstinately behind as you pulled the shells out. We would often have to submerge ourselves, and run out of breath in the tussle, but, cold and wet, we would return home triumphantly to grill our booty on top of the stove and eat them simply – with freshly ground pepper (no salt was needed) – as soon as they opened.

Mussels are popular in Venice as they are so freely available – both farmed and wild. They are served in soups, in *antipasti*, in seafood salads, *fritto misto*, and in fish stews. They are delicious in the following soup, but many other small crustaceans may be cooked similarly.

Cleaning mussels is always a laborious task, but since there's no avoiding it you just have to roll up your sleeves and get on with it. Each one should be washed under cold running water and scrubbed with a brush. Pull out as much of the beard as you can, and cut off the rest with a sharp knife. Discard any mussels that are not tightly closed (or do not immediately close when sharply tapped with a knife) and also any that feel heavier than the rest or give out any sludge or slime. Finally, put them in a bowl of cold water and carefully examine any that float; if they are open even a tiny crack you must discard these as well. It goes without saying that if you have bought them as fresh as possible from a good fishmonger, there should be few rejects.

Although they can be kept under certain conditions, you ought to plan to cook mussels on the day you buy them. You will be relieved to learn that cleaning is by far the hardest part, cooking them is very simple!

ZUPPA DI COZZE

◆

Mussel Soup

SERVES 2
1 lb fresh, cleaned mussels
extra virgin olive oil

2 garlic cloves, halved
a dash of white wine
1¼ cups tomato sauce (see page 87)

In a large, deep pot pour enough olive oil to cover the bottom, heat gently and brown the garlic slowly. Add the mussels, cover the pot and cook on a high flame, shaking the pot from time to time. Add the wine and continue cooking as before until the mussels have opened.

Add the tomato sauce and heat through, then pour into two large bowls, shells and all, and serve at once, eating the mussels with your fingers and the juices with a spoon. This dish is so good that it might be wise to buy double the quantity of mussels so you can start again from the beginning.

As such a huge variety of fish and shellfish is caught in the Adriatic, there are many recipes which use them all together, such as this soup and the stew on page 132. These would both be favorites with amateur fishermen since, as they come home with so many different types of seafood, a mixed dish is the obvious answer. A good place to try a *zuppa di pesce*, not dissimilar to the one below, is Do Forni or Graspo de Ua, the latter one of the oldest established restaurants in Venice (similar in style to Simpsons in the Strand or Maxims in Paris). Their menu is extensive, not exclusively Venetian, but full of good things all the same, particularly their fish soup – not always listed as such on the menu, but truly delicious. One word of warning, however: when you order this they will bring you a big red bib and make a great show of tucking it into your shirtfront. This is so the delectable juices from the fish and shellfish will not ruin your outfit and is surely well meant, but sensitive souls may feel a little uncomfortable kitted out rather like a dentist's victim!

The kitchen at Da Romano in Burano.

BRODETTO DI PESCE

Fish Soup

SERVES 6
4½ lb assorted fish (eel, monkfish,
   shrimp, mussels, squid)
extra virgin olive oil
1 onion, finely sliced
3 garlic cloves, finely chopped

½ cup dry white wine
scant cup tomato sauce (see
   page 87)
finely chopped parsley
salt and pepper

Clean and wash the eel and cut this and the monkfish into largish pieces. Prepare the shrimp, mussels and squid.

Pour a generous amount of olive oil into a deep pan and sweat the onion and garlic until they begin to take on a little color. Add all the fish and the wine, cover tightly and cook gently for 30 minutes.

Add the tomato sauce, parsley and seasoning to taste, and cook, covered, for 30 minutes more. Serve in soup bowls with *crostini di pane*, rounds of French bread toasted or fried in a little butter.

In Venice, restaurants will almost always offer *antipasti* of fish, which might include a dish like Gambaretti con Fagioli. In the Veneto we would make this with tiny, sweet Adriatic small shrimp and fresh *cannellini* beans, but you can approximate the flavor using canned *cannellini* and the best small, fresh shrimps you can find.

GAMBARETTI CON FAGIOLI

◆

Fresh Small Shrimp with Beans

SERVES 4
1 lb fresh small shrimp
a small piece each of carrot and celery
1½ cups canned *cannellini* beans
a few leaves of arugula

2 garlic cloves, finely chopped
extra virgin olive oil
lemon juice
salt and pepper

Wash the shrimp in running water. Put the carrot and celery in a pan of water and bring to the boil. Add the shrimp and boil rapidly – they should take no more than 3 minutes to cook, less if they are very small.

As soon as the shrimp are cool enough to handle, shell them and put them in a serving dish. Drain the beans well in a colander and add to the shrimp, together with the arugula, torn into small pieces, and the garlic. Dress with some oil, lemon juice, and salt and pepper to taste, mix well, and leave to marinate for up to an hour – try to serve the dish while it is still slightly warm.

Gambaretti are a particular Venetian speciality, and a familiar sight used to be whole families – including children and grandparents – cooking, peeling and selling the tiny pink shellfish in the street. This recipe is my version of a dish cooked all along the Adriatic coast, using shrimp. These must be very fresh and juicy, so do not attempt to make this dish if you have only frozen shrimp. Quantities are not crucial, and depending on the size of the shrimp, and how many you have, you can serve this as an *antipasto* or a main course – 5–6 medium shrimp per person for the latter perhaps, along with the other ingredients.

SPIEDINI DI GAMBERONI

◆

Shrimp Brochettes

fresh Mediterranean or jumbo shrimp
fat bacon, ideally *pancetta*, cut into
  pieces
some leaves of fresh sage
some sprigs of rosemary

home-made breadcrumbs
finely diced garlic
finely chopped parsley
butter

Preheat the broiler until it is red-hot. Shell the shrimp, leaving the heads and tails on, and remove the black intestinal tract. Thread them on to fine skewers, alternating with a piece of bacon, a leaf of sage and a sprig of rosemary (which you can loop around the skewer and catch in a little knot).

Put the skewers under the very hot broiler and cook for a few minutes, turning once. Mix the breadcrumbs with half the garlic and parsley, and sprinkle over the shrimp. Return to the broiler just long enough for the crumbs to brown.

Meanwhile melt the butter gently with the rest of the garlic and parsley. When the *spiedini* are cooked, put them on a platter and pour the melted flavored butter over the shrimp. Serve at once.

Another Venetian *antipasto* dish consists of 'sweet and sour' sardines. They have been prepared like this in Venice since the Middle Ages and are an excellent example of the ingenuity and thriftiness of medieval cooks – using only sardines and onions you could prepare them today and eat them in 3 months' time. Elsewhere you may come across recipes which include raisins, *pinoli* (pine kernels or nuts) and capers, but all you really need to make this tasty dish are the ingredients opposite.

SARDINE IN SAOR

Sweet and Sour Sardines

SERVES 6
a good 2 lb fresh sardines
a little all-purpose flour
olive oil

1 lb onions, sliced very, very finely
wine vinegar
salt and pepper

Snap the heads off the sardines and at the same time pull out the intestines. Scale them as best you can with a sharp knife, rinse well under cold running water, and pat dry with kitchen paper. Roll them in flour, shake off the excess and fry in hot oil a few at a time, turning them once and draining on kitchen towels when cooked.

In a separate pan, gently heat some more oil and fry the onion until it is just transparent.

In a large container – an earthenware pot is ideal – place a layer of sardines. Cover with a layer of onion, add a few drops of vinegar, and little salt and pepper. Add another layer of sardines, cover with onion, add vinegar and seasoning, and continue in this manner until all the ingredients are used up, finishing with an onion layer. Cover with a lid and leave to marinate for at least 12 hours before serving.

Another typical use of the multitude of seafood available in the Veneto is in a salad. Any seafood salad should be an interesting mixture of tastes and textures, so try to include as many different types of seafood as possible. Quantities depend on what you can get and whether you want to serve the salad as *antipasto* or main course.

INSALATA DI MARE

◆

Seafood Salad

seafood: octopus, squid, mussels, clams, scallops and small shrimp
salt and pepper
carrot
onion

vinegar
finely chopped garlic to taste
finely chopped parsley
the very best extra virgin olive oil
lemon juice

Cut the tentacles from the octopus and, if it was a large one, beat them violently with a steak beater or, failing that, an ordinary hammer (you can wrap the head in a plastic bag if the latter is dirty). Remove any scales still attached to the suckers and drop the tentacles for a moment into boiling water. Blanch them quickly, then skin them and cut into rings.

Hold the squid under running water and pull out the beak and the ink sac. Turn the body inside out to wash away any residue (this is not quite so ghastly in practice as it sounds). If the squid is quite large, continue holding it under running water while you peel off the skin from the tentacles and body, then cut it all into rings. If small, remove as much skin as you can and leave whole.

Clean the mussels, clams and scallops as described on pages 113, 57 and 124 respectively. Rinse the small shrimp under running water but do not shell them.

In three separate pans, each containing lightly salted water, a little carrot and some onion, cook the octopus, squid and shrimp. The squid will take 20 minutes or so on a gentle boil, the octopus nearer 40, but test both towards the end of the cooking time and remove at once as soon as they are tender. The little shrimp will only take a moment once the water has returned to a fast boil. Drain and shell them.

Drop the scallops into boiling salted water to which you have added a few drops of vinegar. Return to the boil for a couple of minutes, drain and cut into slices.

Put the mussels and clams into two heavy-bottomed pans with just the drops of water remaining from cleaning. Put on a high flame and shake vigorously for a few minutes, with a tight lid on each pan. After a moment check whether all the shells have opened. If not, replace the lids and continue shaking the pans for a moment or two more. When cool enough to handle, shuck the mussels and clams.

Put all the seafood into a serving bowl, add the garlic and parsley (as much or as little of both as you like), and dress with oil, lemon juice, salt and pepper. Leave to marinate for 2 hours and serve at room temperature.

A popular dish on the Santini menu is cuttlefish cooked in their own ink (a *risotto* using the ink is equally popular, see page 74). This dish is very Venetian, but there we use the very smallest fish, not so commonly available here. Use the smallest you can find.

SEPPIE CON NERO

Cuttlefish in their Ink

SERVES 4

$2\frac{1}{4}$ lb tiny cuttlefish, with ink
extra virgin olive oil
1 onion, finely sliced
1 garlic clove, halved
$\frac{1}{2}$ cup white wine

salt and pepper
3–4 tomatoes, skinned and chopped, or some home-made tomato sauce (see page 87) (optional)

Clean the cuttlefish very carefully. You must remove the beak and then detach the ink sac from the head without breaking it. Put the ink sacs into a bowl and then proceed to clean out the body, in the manner described for squid opposite.

One of my favorite lunchtime restaurants in Venice is La Madonna,
where the display of seafood on offer is mouth-watering.

In a pan about 4 inches deep, heat a little olive oil and sweat the finely sliced
onion and the garlic for a few minutes until soft. Add the cuttlefish, cut into rings if
they are on the large side, but best if tiny and left whole. Toss them for a minute or
two in the oil, then add the dry white wine. Allow this to bubble up, then cover the
fish with water. Season and add, if you wish, some tomato or tomato sauce. Allow this
to cook gently while you prepare the ink sacs.

Pour a little warm water into the bowl containing the ink sacs and break each sac
with the point of a knife. Mix the ink and the water and pass through a colander into a
second bowl.

Turn up the heat under the cuttlefish until most of the liquid has evaporated,
then add the ink. Turn the heat down to very low and cook for $1\frac{1}{2}$–2 hours, uncovered,
to allow the ink to reduce to a rich sauce and the cuttlefish to become tender.

Seppie con Nero – tiny cuttlefish braised in their own ink (page 121), served here with *polenta* – makes a wonderful main course as served at L'Incontro.

Seafood is not presented in Italy as it is in northern France – cooked plainly and simply (or left raw) and displayed beautifully on huge platters. This is seafood for the true *aficionado*, and most Italians, myself included, would prefer it with a good sauce to dip into, or simply some extra virgin olive oil. The Italian way, of course, is basically *as* simple, but with a little flavoring added. The next recipe is just such an *antipasto* dish – my own – using the best and freshest ingredients, and without masking the fresh flavors. The scallops must be very fresh and in their shells because the success of the dish rests on the delicate juices given out by the shellfish during cooking.

CAPPE SANTE

Baked Scallops

PER PERSON
2–3 fresh sea scallops, in their shells
a little extra virgin olive oil
a dash of paprika sauce

a squeeze of lemon juice
salt and pepper
2–3 thin slices of onion
a dash of white wine

Preheat the oven to 400°F.

Open the scallop shells and with a very sharp knife cut the shellfish as cleanly as possible away from the flat half of the shell. Rinse and clean them, removing the black intestinal thread and the 'skirt' which attaches them to the shell.

Put each scallop into the rounder half of its shell, add a few drops of olive oil, a dash of paprika sauce, a squeeze of lemon juice, some salt and pepper and an onion slice. Place on a rack in the preheated oven for 5 minutes, then add a drop of white wine to each shell. Replace for about 5 minutes more, just long enough for the scallops to color, then remove to a plate and serve at once.

A simple recipe for sole is ideal for a dinner party. All the preparation can have been done well in advance, and then when you're almost ready to serve – in one dish or individual plates – the fish can be popped into the preheated oven for a few moments. Use fillets of Dover sole, which are much larger than the sole of the Adriatic.

FILETTI DI SOGLIOLA AL BASILICO

Sole with Basil

SERVES 4
a good 1¼ lb fresh sole fillets
extra virgin olive oil
2 medium Italian plum tomatoes,
   fresh or canned, sliced

butter
salt and pepper
a dash of white wine
several leaves of fresh basil

Preheat the oven to 400°F. Rinse the fish in cold running water and pat dry. Pour a tiny amount of olive oil in a gratin dish, tilting the dish so the oil covers the bottom completely. Put the fish in a single layer in the gratin dish, with some slices of tomatoes on each fillet and a good knob of butter. Add a little salt and pepper and pour some olive oil over the top.

Put them in a preheated oven for 6–7 minutes, then add some white wine and cook for a few moments more. Tear the basil leaves into pieces and sprinkle over the sole just before serving.

Fish in Italy is generally fried, broiled or boiled – cooked in a simple way. which cannot be bettered if the fish is wonderfully fresh. Monkfish is now one of the most popular fish in Italy and France, and is imported from all over the world to keep up with the demand. It has become quite expensive, but I can remember not very long ago when it was so looked down on – it's very ugly to look at – that it was thrown away! *Coda di rospo* can be broiled and moistened with a little melted butter, garlic and parsley, but you may like to try this recipe which is easy to prepare and very tasty. The same method and ingredients can be used for other fish, but they should be filleted first, to get rid of the bones. Mackerel, for instance, would be delicious prepared this way, as would tuna.

CODA DI ROSPO SANTA BARBARA

Monkfish with Peppers and Carrots

SERVES 4
4 monkfish steaks
1½ onions
extra virgin olive oil

good ½ cup tomato sauce (see page 87)
salt and pepper
2 carrots, scrubbed and finely sliced
1 red pepper, cleaned and diced

Dice the half onion and fry gently in some oil in a pan large enough to hold all the fish in a single layer. When softened, add the monkfish steaks and fry for a moment, making sure they don't stick. Add the tomato sauce and a little salt and pepper, and

Coda di Rospo Santa Barbara – monkfish with
peppers and carrots (page 125) a Santini speciality, is light and delicious.

At home, before starting to prepare a *Fritto Miso* – deep fried mixed
fish (page 128) – I gather together all the raw ingredients.

cook over medium heat, covered, for 5 minutes, then carefully turn the monkfish over and cook, uncovered, for 5 minutes more.

Meanwhile, slice the rest of the onion, and heat a little oil in another skillet. Sauté the onion, carrot and pepper for a moment or two. Remove from the heat while they are still crunchy. Drain the oil from them, and serve the monkfish directly onto four warmed plates with a little of the cooking sauce and the vegetables poured over the top. Accompany with some cooked vegetables in season, and a little mashed or boiled potato.

A *fritto misto* is the most popular way of preparing fish in Venice. Small fish and shellfish are used – the fish from the Adriatic are small in general – and you should allow roughly $\frac{3}{4}$ lb weight per person for a main course. Do try to have as good a variety of seafood as possible.

A *fritto misto* is a little tricky to make at home but well worthwhile for the more experienced cook. Since it is rather complicated and time-consuming, you may decide it's worth preparing rather a lot of fish in this manner and inviting several guests to enjoy an unusual and informal meal.

FRITTO MISTO
◆
Deep-fried Mixed Fish

fish and shellfish (cuttlefish; squid; shrimp or *schie*; scallops; fresh anchovies, sardines or whitebait; large shrimp; firm white fish such as monkfish or sole)

vegetable oil for frying
all-purpose flour
salt

Prepare and cook the cuttlefish, squid, shrimps and scallops as described on pages 120–124. Prepare the shrimp in the same way as the shrimps, cooking them for a few minutes longer and removing the black intestinal tract after peeling. This stage can be carried out in advance and the cooked shellfish refrigerated until needed. Allow them to come to room temperature before frying.

Clean the anchovies and sardines as on page 119; wash the whitebait in cold running water and pat dry. Cut the firm white fish into thin strips.

Put a deep, heavy-bottomed pan on to heat, filling it one-third full of vegetable oil (*not* olive). Meanwhile coat all the fish and shellfish in flour and place in a dry colander to shake off the excess flour. (Many recipes suggest using batters for *fritto misto*; I prefer simply flour.)

Drop a small shrimp in the oil; if it bubbles and browns immediately the oil is ready. Begin with the cuttlefish and squid, taking care not to put too many pieces into the pan at once. Take out the fish as it cooks and turns a golden brown, adding more pieces so that the oil remains at an even temperature. Put the cooked fish in a large roasting pan which you have lined with several sheets of newspaper, with a top layer of paper towels. Keep this in a warm place, removing the drained fish to a plate if the pan is crowded. If you are preparing a lot of fish and the paper becomes very oily, ask someone to change it while you continue to fry the fish.

Follow the cuttlefish and squid with the anchovies and sardines, the large shrimp, white fish, the scallops, the whitebait, and finally the shrimp, draining and removing to the warm paper-covered pan.

When all the frying is completed, turn off the heat, arrange all the drained fish on a serving platter, sprinkle with salt, and serve with some slices of *polenta* you have kept warm in a slow oven (see page 102) a mixed green salad and a plate of lemon wedges. You will also need plenty of chilled white wine with which to toast the cook.

A similar dish to Fritto Misto is Grigliata di Pesce, which is popular along the Adriatic coast. Before the advent of electric ventilation, this was always a speciality of the summer restaurants which could move the kitchen outdoors and broil the day's catch over charcoal. I recommend you do the same because, although it tastes wonderful, it doesn't smell very nice when cooked indoors.

For a *grigliata*, you need quite robust fish which won't fall into pieces while cooking. Good choices are monkfish, sole, langoustine, small red mullet, squid, cuttlefish and jumbo shrimp. As far as quantities are concerned, a 'piece' of each fish should do per person – one large piece monkfish, one langoustine, one red mullet and so on.

GRIGLIATA DI PESCE

◆

Broiled Fish

fish and shellfish, as on page 128
finely chopped garlic
finely chopped parsley

fresh breadcrumbs
extra virgin olive oil
salt and pepper

Wash the fish and cut into largish pieces. Clean the squid and cuttlefish as described on pages 120 and 121; wash the langoustines, or jumbo shrimp and the shrimp.

To prepare a *pestato*, mix the chopped garlic and parsley together, and then add the breadcrumbs, olive oil and some salt and pepper. For rough proportions put 2 inch parsley, garlic and breadcrumbs into a cup and fill up with olive oil. The consistency should be of a light soup such as *stracciatella*. Have this ready in a bowl with a pastry brush near where you are going to cook the fish.

Pour a few drops of olive oil, not too much, over the fish, sprinkle with salt and pepper, and cook over medium heat, turning once. Add the bigger pieces of fish first – monkfish, mullet, cuttlefish, langoustine, or jumbo shrimp. It's difficult to give a precise timing, so watch the fish carefully and don't overcook it. When done, remove to a warm plate and brush with the *pestato*. The flavor of the oil, which has soaked into the breadcrumbs, remains *on* the fish, rather than running off. Delicious and deliciously simple, to be accompanied only by a salad.

Eel is another fish much loved and used in the Veneto, coming from the rivers flowing across the plain into the Adriatic, and from a natural 'tank' in the Laguna. Hungry local fishermen catch eel in a special hand-clasp so that they can't wriggle away, suspend them from the head and then open them with one slash from top to bottom and remove the bones. The eel is then cut into five or six pieces, put on to a hot wood-fired broiler and cooked with just a little salt and pepper. The skin isn't eaten, but as this is very fatty, it moistens and protects the soft white flesh. Simple and beautiful.

This is my own recipe for eel in which all the ingredients are cooked together to make a most delicious sauce. You might also care to try it with a good free-range chicken. This recipe does not call for the fish to be cooked in a *soffritto* – the softened combination of onion, garlic and oil – instead the onion and garlic are added raw to the pan and their flavors permeate the eel (or the chicken) in a very subtle yet tasty way. A medium eel should be enough for 3–4 people, for the sauce expands the dish quite considerably. My brother never liked eel at home, but he was quite happy eating a helping of the sauce along with the *polenta*!

ANGUILLA IN UMIDO

Braised Eel

SERVES 3–4
1 medium eel
1 onion, diced
2 garlic cloves, diced
a few fresh rosemary leaves

1 bay leaf
a few black peppercorns
$\frac{1}{2}$ cup white wine
2–3 tomatoes, skinned and chopped
olive oil

Clean and wash the eel and remove its head. Make a number of diagonal incisions along the back, taking care not to cut right through the flesh. This dish is at its best when cooked in a round terracotta pot – the eel is wound around the bottom in a coil in one layer and should fit snugly but not too tightly on the bottom of the pot.

Add all the remaining ingredients to the pot with the eel, along with a good measure of olive oil, put over a low heat, and cook, covered tightly, for an hour. At the end of this time check for seasoning and if the eel is not completely tender continue to cook, still covered and still on gentle heat, for half an hour longer.

The eel is ready when, by pressing lightly across the cut parts, the flesh falls into serving pieces. Serve it in its sauce with soft *polenta* (see page 102). It is quite beautiful.

In Jesolo (my home town) during the Second World War, the beach was totally mined by the Germans, as was the sea, so there was no fishing for years. After the war, the mines had to be got rid of – many in the sea were already encrusted with mussels – and almost daily there were tons of fish floating on the surface of the sea after the mines were exploded. At first, we all revelled in this – food had been short – and we had fish for breakfast, lunch and dinner, fried, broiled or in stews like the following. But it all palled after a while – over-indulgence does put you off!

This is my own recipe for a fish stew, but it is very characteristic of the Veneto, and is similar to the preceding eel recipe in that all the ingredients are cooked together to make a good sauce. You can choose whichever fish you prefer, but I would suggest a selection as below.

TECCIADA DI PESCE

Fish Stew

PER PERSON
seafood: choose from 1 small red
   mullet, 1 small striped bass, 1 piece
   of monkfish, 1 piece of eel,
   1 langoustine or jumbo shrimp,
   1 shelled sea scallop. 3–4 mussels,
   1 small squid. Allow at least $\frac{3}{4}$ lb fish
   or shellfish per person (including
   shells)

1 potato, sliced
$\frac{1}{2}$ onion, diced
$\frac{1}{2}$ garlic clove, diced
a few rosemary leaves
1 bay leaf
a few black peppercorns
extra virgin olive oil
white wine
1 tomato, chopped

Clean the squid and the mussels as described on pages 120 and 113. Split the langoustine in half and remove the black intestinal tract. Clean and wash the rest of the fish.

Put all the fish in a roasting pan large enough to accommodate everything in one layer, and add all the remaining ingredients. Cover the top tightly with foil and put in a cool oven – about 275°F – for 40 minutes. At the end of this time remove the foil, put the pan on the top of the stove, and cook a while longer to reduce the sauce a little.

The two recipes following are my own, and are not particularly Venetian. They both, however, clearly illustrate my principal philosophy of good, fresh foods being cooked and presented in the simplest possible ways to preserve their quintessential flavors.

Sea bass, and it's near relative, striped bass, that is found in America, to me are two of the best fish in the world, and don't need very much anyway to make them taste good. The sauce – which is best prepared a day in advance so that the flavors mingle – is completely cold, but when it is poured over the steaming bass, it is warmed up slightly. Customers come from all over the world to taste this!

BRANZINO SANTINI
◆
Bass with Herb Sauce

SERVES 4–5

1 striped or sea bass, weighing about 2¾ lb, cleaned and gutted

1 onion, cut into quarters

3 carrots, scraped and left whole

1 bay leaf

1 parsley sprig

salt and pepper

Sauce

generous cup extra virgin olive oil

a good squeeze of lemon juice

½ cup Worcestershire sauce

a large rosemary sprig

½ garlic clove, finely chopped

a small bunch each of chives and parsley, chopped

a few drops balsamic vinegar

a tiny pinch of Aromat seasoning dissolved in a little water

Make the sauce first. Mix the oil, lemon juice and Worcestershire sauce. Strip the leaves from the rosemary stalk and add these, the garlic and the other herbs to the sauce. Mix in the vinegar and dissolved Aromat, and leave in a cool place for at least 24 hours.

Put a large shallow pan of water – a fish kettle if you have one, or a pan out of which the fish can be easily lifted without breaking – on to boil and add all the ingredients except the fish. When the water starts to bubble, turn the heat down very low and put in the fish. Cook gently, with just a slight ripple on the surface of the water, for 10–12 minutes, depending on the size of the fish (longer for a larger fish, but not more than 15 minutes).

People come from all over the world
to enjoy *Branzino Santini*, my speciality
– bass with herb sauce (page 133).

Remove the fish to a serving dish and very carefully lift away the skin from the side uppermost, starting just beneath the gills and ending at the tail. This is a rather fiddly operation, so be patient.

Stir the sauce, which will have separated, to incorporate all the ingredients and pour over the bass. Serve at once with boiled potatoes and a green salad.

This salmon recipe is a new variation on my version of the beef *carpaccio* (see page 156). As for quantities, what you are wanting to do is to have enough very thinly sliced salmon to cover a serving plate per person. It's very simple, quite delicious, and involves virtually no cooking.

SALMONE SANTINI

◆

Salmon with Peppercorns

fresh salmon, whole or a good middle cut, well chilled
salt and pepper
extra virgin olive oil
fresh dill

a few green peppercorns
a few capers, preserved in oil, *not* vinegar (optional)
freshly squeezed lemon juice

Split the whole or piece of salmon in half, and with the point of a knife remove all the little bones. This is very fiddly, but it must be done. Then, taking your sharpest knife, cut fine slices from the salmon as if it were smoked. Don't worry if you can't get them paper-thin because next you must put each slice between two sheets of waxed paper and press down hard to flatten with the heel of your hand.

Arrange the slices in one layer, with none overlapping, to cover the entire surface of a serving plate. Season with a little salt and pepper, sprinkle on some drops of olive oil, and add some dill, green peppercorns and, if you like, some capers.

Leave for 10 minutes so the flavors can mingle then put the plate under a hot broiler for *1 minute only* so the salmon is warmed through, *not* cooked. Sprinkle some lemon juice over it and serve at once.

One of the most characteristic Venetian ingredients is *baccalà*, salt or dried cod – an oddity when the Adriatic has none, and it has to be imported, mostly from Norway – but it is a passion shared by many other countries in Europe, particularly Spain and Portugal. In Italy *baccalà* is a poor man's food, and I put it on my menu at Santini as an experiment only, but it has become one of the most popular dishes.

Salt cod must be soaked for 12 hours before cooking, and for this particular dish, there are further requirements: *baccalà* should be *battuto da un matto e condito da un saggio* – 'beaten by a madman and seasoned by a wise man'!

BACCALÀ MANTECATO

Creamed Salt Cod

SERVES 4
a good 2 lb salt cod
½ onion
1 celery stick

extra virgin olive oil
finely chopped parsley
salt and pepper

Soak the cod in several changes of cold water for at least 12 hours to remove all the salt. Put the cod in a pan of fresh water, adding the onion and celery to flavor it (and reduce the smell) as it cooks. Simmer gently for about 30 minutes, or until the flesh starts to come away from the bones. Allow to cool, then remove the skin and bones.

Put the fish in a bowl and beat it with an egg beater, adding a few drops of olive oil very slowly, then a little more, and so on as if you were making mayonnaise. When it starts to form a mousse, add as much parsley as you like, with a little salt if needed and some pepper. Serve with slices of grilled *polenta* (see page 102).

This dish comes from the Ristorante al Salisa in Conegliano, owned by a friend of mine, passionate about reviving old, traditional dishes.

BACCALÀ ALLA VICENTINA
◆
Gratin of Salt Cod

SERVES 6

2¾ lb salt cod	2 garlic cloves
all-purpose flour	6 anchovies (canned in olive oil)
salt and pepper	2¼ cups each of milk and fish stock
extra virgin olive oil	3 tablespoons tomato sauce (see page 87)
1 onion, finely sliced	1 cup grated Parmesan cheese
½ stick butter	finely chopped fresh parsley

Soak the cod in several changes of cold water for at least 12 hours to remove all the salt. Remove the bones from the soaked cod, but leave the skin on. Dip the fish in a little flour seasoned with salt and pepper, and fry gently on both sides in a little olive oil with the onion. When the fish is golden remove from the pan and take off the skin. Cut this into tiny pieces and scatter over the fish, placed in a baking dish with the onion.

Melt the butter in a pan and fry the garlic cloves, removing them when they become brown. Add the anchovies and sprinkle on 2 tablespoons all-purpose flour, allowing it to cook for a moment. Add a little milk, stirring so the flour is amalgamated, then add the rest, the fish stock and the tomato sauce, along with the garlic cloves. Beat this with a beater, check for seasoning, and pour over the fish to cover it.

Dust over the Parmesan cheese and the chopped parsley and cook in a very slow oven – 275°F, – for 1½ hours. Serve with soft *polenta* (see page 102).

CHAPTER FOUR

Poultry,
Game and Meat

The good farmland of the Veneto provides excellent beef, veal, lamb and pork. The beef is served hot and juicy in Bollito Misto, or stewed or spit-roasted. Veal does not feature as highly in Venetian cooking as in some other regions but calf's liver is prized for the famous Fegato alla Veneziana and other dishes. We also value the kidneys, which are cooked *trifolati*, sliced and sautéed with white wine. Lamb appears roasted and stewed, and the pig is turned into all kinds of ham and salami – the most famous being *soppressa* – while the poorer cuts are used to give taste and substance to soups and bean dishes.

The Veneto has always been famous for its capons, and here chicken does taste of chicken. This is due mainly to the fact that in Italy it is forbidden by law to feed fishmeal to poultry and there is strict control over the use of chemicals and hormones, resulting in birds with tastier, firmer flesh which are also better for you. It's possible to buy a free-range chicken, a *pollo ruspante*, complete with head, legs and all its innards, in any butcher in any town in Italy. The eggs are also much better, with real yellow yolks. There are few turkeys in the Veneto these days, although there used to be little black ones, not much bigger than chickens, which were moist and tasty (unlike the great ostriches bred today).

Goose is a great favorite in the autumn and winter months, served crisply roasted and often accompanied by raw celery 'for the digestion'. Quail, *quaglie*, are popular, either roasted and served with *funghi porcini* or with *risotto*. Guinea hen, *faraona*, is a great speciality, roasted and served with *la peverada*, a peppery sauce of medieval origin. The salt marshes of the Laguna are home to wild duck and other waterfowl, and pigeon nest in towns and woods all over the Veneto.

In the autumn the hunters set out in search of game. They meet early, though usually not *too* early, in a village *trattoria* for some coffee and a nip of something more fortifying, then the local official, who may feel he also needs a little fortifying, allots a different area of the woods to each group to make sure the only casualties are the birds. Pheasant, *fagiano*, partridge, *pernice*, and little birds such as thrushes, *tordi*, are the victims and are served roasted with *polenta* and *funghi porcini*. In the foothills of the Alps hare is also shot and served roasted or jugged. Uncannily, whether the birds have been easy to track down or have remained elusive, the hunters always arrive back at the *trattoria* around lunchtime, and usually in need of some more fortification. . . .

In the following recipe, the spring chicken is broiled, but in the *Terra Ferma* it would be cooked on a spit broiler. Most restaurants have these contraptions inside in full view, holding *spiedini*, mixed meats and a selection of chickens and other little birds, which are often basted with oil on a goose feather. Underneath there may be pans of *polenta* being flavored by the dripping juices in much the same way as a Yorkshire pudding was once flavored beneath a piece of beef.

GALLETTO ALLA DIAVOLA

Grilled Small Chicken

PER PERSON
1 small broiling chicken or *poussin*
extra virgin olive oil

salt and pepper
a pinch of chili pepper
juice of ½ lemon

Cut the chicken along the backbone and open it out with your hands, cracking the breastbone so that it lies as flat as possible. Rub the skin all over with a little oil, some salt, plenty of freshly ground black pepper, and a pinch of chili pepper.

Put the chicken skin side up, under a hot broiler and cook, basting it from time to time with lemon juice. Turn it over, sprinkle a few drops of oil and lemon and some salt, pepper and a further tiny pinch of chili pepper on the inside and continue cooking. Then turn it skin side up again and finish cooking, basting with lemon juice as before. It will cook quite quickly and be juicy and fragrant. (If you can cook it outdoors over charcoal it will be even better.) Serve with salad.

This chicken dish – my own recipe, obviously – can either be broiled or pan-fried. It's very tasty. It's also a worry-free choice for a dinner party as it's quick and healthy, and can be prepared ahead up to the final broiling or frying stage, and stored in the refrigerator.

POLLO SANTINI

Chicken Breast with Mustard

SERVES 4
4 boned chicken breasts
extra virgin olive oil
4 teaspoons Dijon mustard
1 garlic clove, finely chopped

1 large bunch fresh parsley, finely
    chopped
2 tablespoons breadcrumbs
Parmesan cheese, freshly grated
salt and pepper

Flatten the chicken breasts as much as you can, then fry gently in some olive oil for 2 minutes on each side. Remove from the pan.

The Lazzarini brothers, very good friends of mine,
set off for a day's hunting for game in the countryside at Soligo.

—— *Opposite* ——

Top, Alfredo's in Treviso, one of the best restaurants in the region, serves roasted
tordi, thrushes, with *polenta* and wild mushrooms. *Below*: One of my favorite
Sunday lunches at home is *Pollo in Tecia* (page 144), chicken with mushrooms and
tomatoes.

Thin the mustard with a little oil, then spread this over one side of each chicken breast. Mix together the garlic, parsley, breadcrumbs and Parmesan, and season with salt and pepper. Sprinkle this over the mustard and continue cooking in the pan or under a hot broiler – another 3–5 minutes or so.

Serve with a pat of butter on the top, or with a buttery pan sauce, and 2 lemon wedges per plate. Fresh vegetables, such as a spinach dish and some sauté potatoes, would go well.

Pollo in Tecia is the Italian equivalent of Poule au Pot or Coq au Vin, a winter casserole (*tecia* means 'pot' in Venetian) designed to stretch one chicken as far as possible.

In the Veneto this will be made with a good *pollo ruspante*, a farm chicken which has spent its days scratching around for food. The flesh of these birds is robust and flavorful. A factory chicken would be no good for this dish as it would disintegrate during cooking, as well as having a bland flavor overpowered by the sauce. Rabbit or veal can also be cooked this way.

POLLO IN TECIA
◆
Chicken with Mushrooms and Tomatoes

SERVES 4

1 good roasting chicken, preferably free-range, weighing just over 2¼ lb and cut into 8 pieces
1 onion, diced
2 garlic cloves, chopped
extra virgin olive oil

2 large Italian plum tomatoes, fresh or canned, peeled and chopped
3 cups sliced *funghi porcini* (or cultivated mushrooms)
a pinch of mixed herbs
salt and pepper
home-made tomato sauce (see page 87)

In a heavy-bottomed pan large enough to hold all the chicken pieces in one layer, fry the *soffritto* of onion and garlic in a little oil. Add the chicken pieces and brown them a little on both sides. Add the tomatoes and the mushrooms, the herbs and salt and pepper to taste.

Cover with a tight lid and cook over medium heat for about 45 minutes, or until the chicken is tender. Check from time to time and if the sauce is reducing too fast add a little home-made tomato sauce.

Serve piping hot with some freshly made *polenta* (see page 102).

The usual way to roast poultry of any kind is to put a sprig or two of herbs inside the cavity and some salt and pepper on the outside. I find this gives you a bird with a salty skin and a bland flavor. If you use a finely chopped stuffing it permeates the flesh and keeps it moist. This will be easier to prepare if you have a food processor or the sort of electric vegetable chopper the Italians call a *trittatutto*; if you must do it by hand, be patient because it is important that the ingredients are chopped as finely as possible.

In either case begin chopping the herbs and garlic first, then follow with the onion so that the mixture will not be too watery.

The other important difference in these roasting recipes is that the birds are basted with warmed stock, sometimes wine as well, not fat. This has two functions: it replaces the moisture which evaporates as the birds cook, and it improves the quality of the pan juices so they make a far tastier contribution to the final result. This is a very useful trick which I employ for all my roasts, whether meat, game or poultry.

POLLO ARROSTO
◆
Roast Chicken

Prepare a stuffing as for Quaglie con Funghi on the next page, adding a few more fresh rosemary and sage leaves.

Wash and dry the chicken and, using your hand, spread the stuffing all around inside the cavity. (It should coat the sides, not *fill* the cavity.) Put half an onion and a bouquet of fresh herbs inside the bird, pour some olive oil over the outside, then season with a little salt and pepper. Place in a deep pan – not a flat roasting pan – as the chicken will keep a better shape and flavor from the juices which accumulate will be absorbed into the chicken instead of evaporating out into the oven. Tuck a sprig of rosemary here and there in the pan, and roast at 350°F until done – about 45 minutes (but it all obviously depends on the size of the chicken).

You can roast some potatoes around the chicken if there is room, basting these and the chicken with a little stock and the pan juices. These will then make a simple and flavorful sauce. Serve with some kind of fresh vegetable or salad, and some *polenta* (see page 102).

FAGIANO ARROSTO

Roast Pheasant

Stuff and cook a pheasant in the same way as Pollo Arrosto, but add more fresh chopped herbs and a few whole juniper berries to the stuffing. Serve as above.

PERNICE ALLA VENETA

Roast Partridge

Stuff and cook some partridges in the same way as Pollo Arrosto. When they are ready remove from the pan and use the juices – the *fondo* – as the base for a sauce. Slice some wild mushrooms into the pan juices, sauté briefly, then add some stock and a little white wine. Let this bubble for a moment, check for seasoning and serve in a sauceboat with the partridges sitting on a bed of soft *polenta* (see page 102).

QUAGLIE CON FUNGHI

Quail with Mushrooms

The quails in this recipe are stuffed completely with the stuffing, and this gives them a good well-rounded flavor. If you like, instead of serving a *risotto* as a first course, then the quails as a main course, you could serve one simpler course of the quails accompanied by a Risotto con Funghi (see page 71).

SERVES 6

12 quails

several sprigs of rosemary and sage for roasting

4 slices of fat bacon, *pancetta* if possible (optional)

extra virgin olive oil

a little hot chicken stock (see page 66)

4 oz *funghi porcini*

3 garlic cloves

finely chopped parsley

Stuffing

2 large garlic cloves

3 rosemary sprigs

1 large sage sprig

1 large parsley sprig

3 medium onions, roughly chopped

2 vegetable bouillon cubes

salt and pepper

To make the stuffing, process or chop the garlic and herbs very finely. Add the onions and continue chopping, then add the crumbled bouillon cubes and a liberal amount of salt and pepper.

Make sure the quails are completely clean, then chop off the necks and divide the stuffing between them, pressing it well down into the cavity of each bird.

Place the birds in rows in a shallow roasting pan with a sprig of rosemary and sage between each one. If using the bacon, cut it into small pieces and place one between each bird in the same manner. Pour a generous amount of olive oil over the quails, grind some black pepper over them and place in the oven, preheated to 350°F, for 45 minutes, basting occasionally with a ladleful of hot stock.

Meanwhile, rinse the mushrooms in cold water, drain and slice each one into several pieces. Gently brown the garlic in hot oil and add the mushrooms, stirring them a little to prevent sticking. When they begin to throw off a little liquid of their own add a ladleful of hot stock and leave them to cook gently for several minutes, until they are soft and juicy. If there is a lot of liquid left in the pan turn up the heat until it reduces. Add some black pepper and keep warm until needed.

When the quails are ready remove them to a warmed serving dish, pour some of the pan juices into the mushrooms, stirring well, and pour the mixture on to the dish with the quails. Dust a little finely chopped parsley over the mushrooms and serve at once.

The following recipe comes from the Ristorante al Salisa in Conegliano, near Treviso. Conegliano is renowned in a number of respects: the painter Cima comes from there; the famous kitchen company Zoppas is based there, as is the best school of oenology (the study of wines) in Italy. Conegliano is also the home of Prosecco wine. The restaurant is run by a friend, Giorgio Ongaro, and I must admit that I haven't yet visited it (I much admired his previous venture). My friends have eaten there, though, and say it's very good. They're all restaurateurs or hoteliers from the coastal resorts and, because of the seasonal nature of their work, they have about five months of each year in which there's little else for them to do except meet, talk, drink, eat – and try out other people's restaurants. I truly believe that this is why Italian restaurateurs become the best in the world – because of this constant exploration, tasting, testing – and I trust their judgement implicitly!

Anchovy and duck may seem a curious combination, but anchovies are used quite a lot in Venetian cooking. The *peverada* sauce (see page 153) often contains a few anchovies, for instance.

ANATRA AL FORNO

Duck with Anchovy Sauce

SERVES 6

1 duck, weighing about $3\frac{1}{4}$ lb

2 tablespoons butter

$\frac{1}{2}$ cup diced bacon or *pancetta*

3 fresh sage leaves

3 rosemary sprigs

3 thyme sprigs

grated zest of 1 lemon

salt and pepper

some good chicken stock (see page 66)

dry white wine

2 garlic cloves, diced

2 tablespoons extra virgin olive oil

3 anchovies

$\frac{1}{4}$ cup diced *soppressa* (salami from the Veneto), or any Italian salami

1 tablespoon white wine vinegar

Wash and dry the duck. Melt the butter in a casserole and fry the bacon and herbs. Add the duck, sprinkle the lemon zest over it, with some salt and pepper, and brown it nicely on all sides. Transfer to a roasting pan and cook in a hot oven at about 350°F for $1\frac{1}{4}$–$1\frac{1}{2}$ hours, basting it from time to time with some stock and white wine.

Meanwhile prepare a sauce by gently frying the garlic in the olive oil. When this is golden add the anchovies and salami, stir well, then add the vinegar and let it reduce gently for 3–4 minutes.

When the duck is ready transfer it to a serving dish and keep warm. Pour off as much fat from the roasting pan as possible and reduce the juices, the *fondo*, on the top of the stove. Add these to the sauce, check for seasoning, and mix briefly in a blender. Serve poured over the duck.

The delicious, satisfying and flavorful *Sopa Coada* – squab soup (opposite) – as served at Da Gigetto, a fine restaurant in Maine, near Valdobbiadene.

Pigeons have been eaten for centuries in the Veneto, and were probably kept for fresh winter meat as they once were in dovecotes in Britain. In Breganze, the pigeons are known as *torresani* (inhabitants of the tower) as they nest in towers there, and people travel from miles around to savour them. They are roasted in the oven or spit-roasted, and cook soft and delicious, never tough.

This Sopa Coada is a very old traditional recipe of the Veneto, and my instinct tells me that it developed as a means of using leftover pigeon – the combination of pigeon meat pieces, bread and broth. It's a rich, hearty dish which needs very slow cooking. It's perfect for supper on a cold wintry day.

SOPA COADA

Squab Soup

SERVES 4

2 squab, cleaned and cut into
  quarters
1 celery stalk, diced
1 carrot, diced
1 onion, finely sliced
butter
$\frac{1}{2}$ cup dry white wine

salt and pepper
7 cups good chicken stock (see
  page 66)
3 chicken livers, cleaned, washed and
  halved
6 slices good rustic bread
grated Parmesan cheese

Fry the celery, carrot and onion in a little butter until golden. Transfer to a large soup pan and add the squab pieces in one layer. Cook these over gentle heat and add the wine little by little, allowing it to reduce into a sauce. Add salt and pepper, cover and continue to cook very gently, adding a little stock as the sauce reduces further. Finally add the chicken livers with a little more stock and cook for a few minutes more. Remove from the heat and, as soon as the squab is cool enough to handle, take out all the bones, keeping the flesh in as large pieces as possible. Remove the chicken livers and set to one side. Add $4\frac{1}{2}$ cups of the chicken stock to the sauce.

Butter a deep-sided oven dish, soak 2 slices of bread in the stock and sauce mixture, and put side by side on the bottom of the oven dish. Dust with grated Parmesan and cover each with a piece of squab and one of chicken liver. Soak 2 more pieces of bread as before, put this over the others, dust with Parmesan, add 2 more pieces of squab and chicken liver, and make a third layer in the same manner.

Pour the remainder of the broth and sauce mixture over the squab and place in a slow oven – at about 325°F – for 5 hours. Check it from time to time and add the remaining broth as necessary. The dish will dry out as it cooks and it is important that the sauce does not reduce too much: it should always remain juicy and soft, rather like *risotto*.

Guinea hen with *la peverada*, a pepper sauce, is a very common recipe in the Veneto, appearing on a great number of menus. It's a good bird to use: a little more solid than chicken, but less tough than pheasant.

Peverada is a descendant of the medieval Venetian sauce *peverata*, and some recipes still include ingredients such as anchovies, ginger and pomegranate juice. This recipe is simpler and lighter, in keeping with today's taste. A vital ingredient of the *peverada* is the liver of the guinea hen, but this may not be easy to come by. If so, you must use chicken livers instead.

FARAONA CON LA PEVERADA
◆
Guinea Hen with Pepper Sauce

SERVES 2–3

1 guinea hen	*Stuffing*
extra virgin olive oil	2 garlic cloves
white wine	2 rosemary sprigs
good chicken stock (see page 66)	1 parsley sprig
	2 onions, roughly chopped
	1 vegetable bouillon cube

Prepare the stuffing for the guinea hen, adding a little salt and pepper, as described in the quail recipe on page 147.

Wash the bird inside and out and pat dry. Stuff the bird, pour some olive oil over it and roast at 350°F for 45 minutes, basting occasionally with a little wine and stock. Meanwhile, make the *peverada*.

Peverada

¼ cup chopped Italian salami, ideally *soppressa* from the Veneto

2 oz chicken livers, or chicken and guinea hen livers

2 garlic cloves

1 parsley sprig

1 teaspoon grated lemon zest

½ cup home-made breadcrumbs

extra virgin olive oil

lemon juice

white wine

salt and freshly ground black pepper

Grind together the salami, chicken livers, 1 garlic clove and the parsley. Put in a bowl and mix in the lemon zest and breadcrumbs. Fry the remaining clove of garlic in a little olive oil until it browns, then remove and discard it. Cook the salami mixture in the garlic-flavored oil, stirring it with a wooden spoon, and moisten with some drops of lemon juice and some white wine. Add a little salt and plenty of freshly ground black pepper and serve in a sauceboat to accompany the guinea fowl.

LEPRE CON PEVERADA

Hare with Pepper Sauce

Make the *peverada* as described above, using the hare liver if you can get it. If not, use chicken livers only.

SERVES 6–8

peverada (see above)

1 hare, weighing about 5½ lb

plain flour

2 onions, diced

2 garlic cloves, diced

extra virgin olive oil

good meat stock (see page 66)

Cut the hare into pieces and dust lightly with flour. In a large lidded pan make a *soffritto* of the onion and garlic fried gently in olive oil, then add the pieces of hare and brown on all sides. Pour a generous ladleful of stock over the hare, cover the pan tightly and cook gently on the top of the stove for 2 hours, or until it is tender. Check from time to time and add a little more stock, but keep tightly covered throughout

Guinea hen with *peverada* (pages 152–3), a traditional and very ancient Venetian sauce, is served with *polenta* at Da Gigetto.

the cooking period. When the hare is almost done, remove the lid and cook over medium heat to reduce the pan juices.

Transfer the hare to a warm serving plate and pour the juices into the *peverada*. Mix well and serve in a sauceboat, with the hare and some soft *polenta* (see page 102).

When visiting Venice, you must visit Torcello, a sleepy little island which has three things to see: a Byzantine church; the Locanda Cipriani (which must be *the* most famous Venetian restaurant after Harry's Bar); and the latest addition, the Ponte del Diavolo, an elegant *osteria* which has become known locally as *ai tre traditori*, 'the three traitors', since three loyal employees of the Cipriani moved a little farther down the canal to open their own restaurant.

Why I mention Torcello here is that *carpaccio* – those very thin slices of fillet of beef pounded flat and served raw – was invented by a

An alternative way of serving *carpaccio*, the raw fillet of beef dish invented in Venice, is as at L'Incontro – with curls of Parmesan and a rocket salad.

chef at the Cipriani, thus it is at heart a very Venetian dish. It is named, obviously, after the Venetian painter, and is normally served brushed with vinaigrette and topped with parsley, chives and capers. This is my *own* version of it, with the arugula adding a wonderful flavor. If arugula is not in season, zucchini make an excellent alternative, but I'm glad to see that arugula is gradually becoming more widely available in markets and supermarkets.

Serve the *carpaccio* in smaller quantities as an *antipasto*, or as a main course as here, with a salad.

CARPACCIO SANTINI 'ROBESPIERRE'

◆

Beef with Arugula

PER PERSON
a scant ½ lb fillet steak
a small bunch of arugula, or 1 medium
  zucchini

butter
salt and pepper
extra virgin olive oil

If using zucchini, cut them into very fine matchsticks and fry very gently in butter for a moment or two.

Slice the steak very finely, as if you were slicing ham, and pound flat. Fillet is very fragile, so do it with your hand, or with very delicate strokes of a wooden mallet.

Arrange the slices to cover the surface of a serving plate, but do not allow any to overlap. Add a sprinkling of salt, a little pepper, and a generous amount of olive oil.

If using arugula, tear into small pieces and sprinkle over the meat – or arrange the zucchini matchsticks to cover the meat.

Put the plate under broiler for 1 minute, until the fillet is just colored. Serve at once.

Italians eat a lot of steak, often cooked rather plainly, so I thought I'd include the following recipe – although it's far from plain!

MEDAGLIONE SANTINI

Beef in Mustard Sauce

SERVES 4

4 *medaglione* (small fillet steaks or
   tournedos)
extra virgin olive oil
a knob of butter
salt and pepper

a dash of brandy

Sauce
4 teaspoons Dijon mustard
1 cup light cream
a dash of Worcestershire sauce

Make the sauce by simply mixing the mustard with the cream and Worcestershire sauce.

Fry the *medaglione* gently in a little oil, turning them once. Calculate the cooking time to your taste and when they are half-way done, pour the oil from the pan and add a knob of butter. When this has melted add the mustard sauce, season with salt and pepper, and finish cooking.

At the last moment add a dash of brandy, flaming it if you like. Serve with a green vegetable like spinach and some sauté potatoes.

Veal is the most popular meat in Italy, and a favorite method of cooking it is as *scallopine di vitello*, small escalopes. As with pasta or *risotto*, there are any number of ways in which the *scallopine* can be flavoured after their basic cooking. Veal is, after all, rather bland, so will accept any kind of sauce.

Basically, for 2 people, cut 8 oz veal across the grain into 6 fine *scaloppine*. Use top round if you can find a butcher who sells it. Beat them flat, bearing in mind that they shrink by a third when cooked. There must be at least three per portion. They should then be dusted with flour, but dust only two out of every three *scaloppine* you are using, shaking off the excess. This will avoid too much flour sticking to the pan and making your sauce stodgy. They should then be fried in a little butter or olive oil until nicely browned on both sides – about $1\frac{1}{2}$ minutes per side. Pour all the fat from the pan and proceed to make your sauce, with the *scaloppine* still in the pan.

The recipe following is one of my own, and slightly more complicated, but the *scaloppine* are cooked in the simple basic way, as are all the variations following.

SCALOPPINE SANTINI

Veal Scallops with Cheese and Mushrooms

SERVES 2

½ lb veal, cut across the grain into 6 fine *scaloppine*

2 cups sliced *funghi porcini*

1 small garlic clove, finely diced

a little finely chopped parsley

4 slices onion, finely diced

extra virgin olive oil

butter

6 thin slices Fontina cheese, cut to fit the *scaloppine* (if unavailable, substitute Gouda)

Cook the mushrooms, garlic, parsley and onion in a little oil over medium heat for 5 minutes, turning up the heat towards the end to reduce the liquid thrown off by the mushrooms.

Lightly flour the *scaloppine* (see page 157), shake off the excess and fry in butter until nicely browned on both sides.

Remove the cooked *scaloppine* to a plate and divide the mushroom mixture between them, spreading it evenly. Cover each one with a slice of Fontina and slide under a hot broiler for a few seconds, just long enough for the cheese to soften a little. Serve at once with a sprinkling of extra parsley. (If you happen to have some tomato sauce available this dish will look very pretty with a spoonful on each *scaloppina* and the parsley dusted over the top.)

SCALOPPINE AL LIMONE (with lemon)

Pour all the oil or butter from the pan and add a knob of butter, a squeeze of lemon juice, some finely chopped parsley and some salt and pepper. Stir well, and serve the *scaloppine* with 2 slices of lemon.

SCALOPPINE CON MANGO (with mango)

Cut a ripe mango in two and blend the pulp from one half (and from the stone) into a purée, cutting the other peeled half into neat slices.

Pour all the oil or butter from the pan, add a knob of butter, the mango purée, some salt and pepper and a little chopped parsley if you like. Warm this very gently through and serve the *scaloppine* garnished with the mango slices.

SCALOPPINE CON POMODORO E BASILICO
(with tomatoes and basil)

Pour all the oil or butter from the pan and in it heat up a little home-made tomato sauce (see page 87). Add some fresh basil leaves torn in pieces, and serve at once.

SCALOPPINE AL ARANCIO (with orange)

Pour all the oil or butter from the pan and add a dash of white wine. Allow it to bubble up for a moment, then add a little salt and pepper, the juice of half an orange, and a knob of butter. Serve with a slice of orange on each *scallopina*.

SCALOPPINE CON FUNGHI (with wild mushrooms)

Pour all the oil or butter from the pan, and warm through some wild mushrooms in it as for Funghi con Polenta (see page 104).

Rolled Breast of Veal is a dish that very few in Britain or America know or appreciate, but it's a very beautiful way to do a roast, and economical too. Have the butcher bone out a piece of breast for you – about $5\frac{1}{2}$ lb for 6 people (a *whole* breast could feed 20 upwards!) – and remove most of the fat. Leave a little to soften and keep the veal moist while it cooks.

PETTO DI VITELLO ARROTOLATO
◆
Rolled Breast of Veal

Open the boned breast out flat and season the inside with salt, pepper, garlic, rosemary and sage leaves and roll it up again (rather like *pancetta*). Tie it neatly and cook it in the oven in a covered pan at 350°F for 2–$2\frac{1}{2}$ hours, glazing it from time to time with white wine and stock, and turning it. The timing is approximate, so test with a skewer to see if the juices are clear. There should be no more than 1 inch of liquid in the bottom of the pan, as you want the veal to roast, not stew. This liquid makes a wonderful sauce.

Towards the end of the cooking time, when it is almost tender, remove the lid and allow the veal to color a little.

The meat is good served hot with some potatoes roasted in the same pan, but it is even better if served cold with salad.

A veal stew is comforting and warming winter food. You can also use breast of veal for this, which is slightly fattier, as the meat should not be too dry. A necessity as an accompaniment is some soft *polenta* or some mashed potato with which you can mop up the flavorful juices.

SPEZZATINI DI VITELLO

Veal Stew

SERVES 4

1½ lb boneless shoulder of veal
1 onion, diced
extra virgin olive oil
a little all-purpose flour
white wine
salt and pepper

home-made meat stock (see page 66)
½ lb *funghi porcini* or cultivated mushrooms
8 oz chopped Italian plum tomatoes, fresh or canned
a few rosemary leaves
1 bay leaf

Cut the excess fat from the veal but leave a little to moisten the meat. Cut the veal into pieces about 1¼–1¾ inches square.

Fry the onion in a casserole in a little olive oil. Dust the meat with flour, shake off the excess and fry gently with the onion. When it is lightly browned on all sides add a dash of white wine, let it bubble up for a moment, then add a little salt and pepper and a couple of ladlefuls of stock. Cover with a tight lid and cook slowly, over medium heat for an hour, checking from time to time and adding a little more stock if necessary.

After the veal has been cooking for about an hour, slice the mushrooms and add these to the pan with the tomatoes, rosemary and bay leaf. Continue to cook, covered, for half an hour more. Check for seasoning, and serve very hot with some freshly made *polenta* (see page 102) or some boiled or mashed potatoes.

Stinco al Forno is my favorite Sunday lunch, and uses shin of veal, the same meat that is cut into pieces for the Milanese *osso buco*. I invented this recipe about 25 years ago when I had a restaurant in Cortina, and it's since become very popular throughout Italy.

STINCO AL FORNO

♦

Braised Shin of Veal

For three people take a whole shin of veal and make about ten holes in it with a sharp knife. Into these put either a sprig of rosemary, a sliver of garlic, a leaf of sage or a little of the finely chopped quail stuffing on page 147.

Put the whole shin into a pan, pour a little olive oil over it, add some salt and pepper and arrange a few potatoes around it, cut into quarters. Cook in a medium oven, at about 325°F for an hour, covered, basting from time to time with a little stock and white wine. Cook a further hour uncovered, continuing to baste and glaze with the pan juices. Use these as a sauce.

You can also cook pork in the same way. It takes less time and produces more fat, therefore omit the potatoes and do not glaze with the pan juices, only with stock and white wine. When it is ready, pour all the fat from the roasting pan and deglaze the juices with some more white wine to serve as a sauce.

Pork is cooked quite a lot in the Veneto, but it is also used in a variety of other ways. When I was working in hotels in Jesolo, I used to 'keep' pigs. Actually they were looked after by a local peasant who would feed them with the hotel kitchen scraps during the summer and then he would be responsible for their feed from October to February, when the hotels were closed. In return for this, we shared the ten pigs fifty-fifty. One February, the man came to me and said he was very sorry, but three of my pigs had died. 'How so,' I asked, 'surely it's $1\frac{1}{2}$ pigs each?' 'No,' was the reply. 'I was saving the best ones for you, and those are the ones that have died'!

February is the month when the pigs are killed, and once again it means a gathering of men, drinking, eating and celebrating. I remember one time with about eight to nine friends when we drank, cooked and ate as we worked: out of some 265–285 lb of pig, which would have made 65 lb of salami, we were left with only enough to make

20 salamis! It sounds a little gruesome, but the fresh meat was delicious, and the whole occasion very enjoyable and sociable.

Among the salamis of the Veneto, *soppressao* is the king. It's a big salami with a much coarser texture than other salamis. It has to be kept for a while, tasting its best after a year, but good *soppressa* is very hard to find now. It like it best with *polenta*: broil a slice of *polenta*, then top it with a slice of *soppressa*. The warmth of the *polenta* melts the fat in the *soppressa* and, served with some wild mushrooms cooked in olive oil, it's a real treat.

Cotecchino is another member of the salami family, and it is made with the fattier parts of the pig, which is why it has to be cooked. It's delicious in Bollito Misto (see page 166). There are also many different kinds of sausage, and I like very much the small spicy ones cooked with Borlotti beans.

SALSICCE DEI FAGIOLI

◆

Sausages and Beans

Prepare the canned beans as for Fagioli all'Uccelletto on page 91, and roast the sausages on top of the stove for 10–15 minutes to get rid of the fat. Drain and put the sausages in with the beans and cook very slowly, covered, for half an hour. A similar dish uses the pig's trotters with lentils: this is traditionally eaten on New Year's Eve, the trotters bringing luck, and the lentils money!

Our bacon for cooking, *pancetta*, I have used in several recipes. It's very like streaky bacon. As always, though, we Italians season it first with pepper and herbs to make it more flavorful. The bacon is rolled up around the seasonings like a salami and left so that the flavors seep through. The meat is quite fatty, but it's cut so thinly to use in cooking – a little thicker than you would cut Parma ham – that as soon as it's put in the pan or the oven, the fat melts immediately. It's very tasty.

The following is a simple recipe for pork or veal cut into cubes to be cooked on skewers under the broiler or on a spit. It would be good barbecued outside too. In dialect *osei scampai* means *uccelli scapati*, or birds that have flown, so called because this is what is used when little game birds, which are cooked in the same way, are not available. You will need to use meat with a little fat of its own, such a pork or slightly fatty veal. I wouldn't recommend beef as it will be too dry.

OSEI SCAMPAI
◆
Pork or Veal Brochettes

pork or veal, cut into 3 inch cubes	fresh sage or bay leaves
bacon or *pancetta*, cut into similar cubes	fresh rosemary sprigs

Thread the ingredients on to long skewers, alternating a piece of meat with one of bacon, a leaf of sage or bay and a rosemary sprig caught into a little knot (as for Spiedini di Gamberoni on page 117). Cook on a spit or under a hot broiler, basting occasionally with the juices, which you can catch in a pan beneath the skewers.

Serve as for game birds, on a bed of soft *polenta* (see page 102), with salad too.

COSTOLETTE DI MAIALE
◆
Pork Ribs

This is the Italian version of Chinese spare ribs. Marinate ribs in a mixture of olive oil, salt, pepper, juniper berries, oregano and any other fresh herbs you like. Leave for about 6 hours, then broil, ideally over charcoal. When they are ready pour the marinade oil over the ribs as a sauce.

Alternatively, use only a little oil in your marinade and cook the ribs, covered, in the oven at about 357°F. Drain the fat from the ribs two or three times and finally, when you have removed as much fat as you can, add a generous dash of white wine. Cook, uncovered, for a few minutes longer to brown the meat.

Lamb is quite popular in Italy, but we eat it when it is very young, virtually milk fed, so it is more a white meat than red. The whole lamb, roasted, is a great speciality at Easter. This following recipe uses tender small cutlets, with a white raisin sauce providing an interesting sweetness.

AGNELLO REGINA

◆

Lamb Cutlets with Sultanas

SERVES 2
6 small lamb cutlets, or rib chops
extra virgin olive oil
a dash of white wine
2 rosemary sprigs

$\frac{1}{3}$ cup white raisins
a large knob of butter
a little finely chopped parsley
$\frac{1}{2}$ ladleful good, home-made meat stock
(see page 66)

Snip through the fat of each cutlet three or four times. This will open out during cooking, keeping the meat flat so that it cooks evenly. Fry the cutlets in a little hot oil, turning them once, until nicely browned, but still pink inside.

Pour off the oil from the pan and add the white wine. Let it bubble up for a moment, then add the chopped rosemary leaves, the white raisins and the butter. When the butter has melted, add the parsley and the stock.

Cook for a moment longer, then remove the cutlets and arrange on two plates. Turn up the heat and allow the sauce to reduce a little, stirring well. Pour over the cutlets and serve at once.

'Mixed boiled meat' sounds very unappetising, and visitors new to Italian cooking are unlikely to choose it from a menu promising more exotic-sounding dishes. If so they will be missing something – a good *bollito* is delicious, the meat soft and tender and full of flavor. It really is as Italian as spaghetti. In some parts of the Veneto it is served with *mostarda da Cremona*, but in Venice we serve it with the following green sauce, as well as with *sott'aceti*, *kren* and coarse salt. *Sott'aceti* are Italian pickled vegetables: cauliflower, carrots, cucumber, etc, all pickled together in flavored vinegar, and they are available in jars. *Kren* is fresh horseradish grated into vinegar: it retains the heat and pungency of the root much more than the milder cream versions.

I cook the different *bollito* ingredients separately because the water from the tongue will not be good, and that from the *cotecchino* will be too fatty. The water from the beef and chicken can be kept to make good stocks, however (and see also page 67 for a traditional use). The important point is that the meat must be put into *boiling* water, so that it seals on contact and keeps all the juices and the flavor inside.

BOLLITO MISTO

Mixed Boiled Meats

SERVES AT LEAST 8

1 *cotecchino* sausage

2¼ lb beef (brisket or chuck) in one
    piece

1 beef tongue, weighing about 2¼ lb

½ calf's head (optional)

1 good chicken

Per individual pot of meat

2 carrots, scraped and left whole

1 large onion, quartered

1 celery stalk

salt

The *cotecchino* should first be soaked in plenty of cold water for several hours. It will take 2½ hours to cook. The beef and tongue will take about 3 hours to cook (more will not hurt). The calf's head, if used, will take about 2 hours, and the chicken 1 hour.

An individual serving of *Bollito Misto*, boiled mixed meats,
with green sauce, horseradish sauce and coarse salt.

Put the vegetables with a little salt into each pan of *cold* water and bring to the
boil. Drop each piece of meat into its respective pan and as soon as the water returns to
the boil, reduce the heat to a gentle simmer. Remove any scum that rises to the surface
and cover each pan. Cook gently, checking from time to time to remove any further
scum.

After 2 hours take out the tongue and remove the outer skin and any gristle, then
return it to the pan. Towards the end of the cooking time you can begin checking the
meat to see if it is done, but do not prick the skin of the *cotecchino* during cooking. If
any meat is ready sooner than anticipated, turn off the heat; it will remain warm
enough to serve for an hour more.

When all the meat is ready remove from the water and slice a little on to each
plate, removing the skin from the *cotecchino* as you do so.

Meanwhile, you will have made the *salsa verde* (overleaf). This is also good with
fish if you substitute lemon juice for the vinegar.

SALSA VERDE

◆

Green Sauce

1 large parsley sprig, finely chopped
½ garlic clove, finely chopped
3 *citrolini* (small dill pickles), finely chopped
a few capers, finely chopped

3 anchovy fillets (canned in olive oil), pounded to a paste
a few drops of wine vinegar
a little extra virgin olive oil
salt and pepper

Put the parsley, garlic, *citrolini*, capers and anchovies in a bowl and mix thoroughly. Add the vinegar, stir well and add the olive oil a little at a time until you reach a sauce-like consistency. Taste and add salt, pepper and more vinegar as necessary.

I love calf's kidneys. When I was growing up in the hotels of my childhood, there weren't many available as we would buy the half calf, thus only one kidney at a time. Once, during the school holidays, when I was about seven or eight, I came down for breakfast, and Elena, the head chef, was preparing the following dish for me. I shall remember that first taste for the rest of my life, and indeed she it was who first gave me a passion for cooking.

ROGNONI TRIFOLATI

◆

Sautéed Kidneys

SERVES 2
2 calf's kidneys
lemon juice or vinegar
extra virgin olive oil

1 garlic clove, diced
white wine
a little finely chopped parsley
salt and pepper

Remove the membrane and any fat from the kidneys. Split them in half and remove the gristle from the core. Put them in cold water with a few drops of lemon juice or vinegar for half an hour. Rinse well under running water. If any odor lingers put them in a dry skillet over very low heat and discard any water than runs out. Rinse again under cold running water and slice very finely.

Heat a little oil in a pan and add the garlic. When it starts to color add the kidneys. Fry quickly, shaking the pan, for a few moments, just long enough for them to lose their raw color. Drain any oil from the pan and add a little white wine, allowing it to bubble up before adding the parsley and some salt and pepper. Serve at once.

No-one really seems to know why liver and onions are so associated with Venice. The combination appears in many cuisines, but it is wonderfully delicate in Venice – perhaps the Venetians invented it!

In order to prepare Fegato alla Veneziana correctly, the liver must be sliced as thinly as possible, no more than $\frac{1}{4}$ in thick. If you are unable to persuade your butcher to do this, you may find it easier to buy the liver in one piece and put it in the freezer for a few hours until it becomes hard enough to slice evenly. If you happen to have a slicing machine at home your job will be made even easier.

The traditional Venetian method is to cook the liver and onions in the same pan. However, I find that if you cook the liver on its own it becomes less 'stewed', and makes for a lighter dish.

FEGATO ALLA VENEZIANA

Calf's Liver and Onions

SERVES 2
$\frac{3}{4}$ lb best calf's liver, thinly sliced
extra virgin olive oil
2 large onions, finely sliced

salt and pepper
a large knob of butter
a little finely chopped parsley

Remove any skin and gristle carefully from the liver slices and discard. Cut the liver meticulously into small pieces about $1\frac{1}{4}$ in square. Dry the pieces well.

Heat some oil in a skillet and cook the onions gently until they soften. Do not allow them to become too brown.

Heat some oil in a separate pan and when it is very hot sauté the liver pieces quickly, turning them once or twice. They should be cooked in no more than a minute. Add a little salt and pepper and pour the liver into the pan containing the onions. Add the butter and parsley and mix well. Serve at once, with a slice of hot *polenta* (see page 102) on each plate.

FEGATO CON SALVIA E SPINACI

◆

Calf's Liver with Sage and Spinach

SERVES 2

¾ lb best calf's liver, sliced as for Fegato alla Veneziana (but not cut into pieces)

extra virgin olive oil
butter
several fresh sage leaves
4 oz raw spinach, washed

Remove any skin and gristle from the liver.

Heat some oil in a skillet and cook the liver very quickly, turning it once.

In a separate pan melt the butter and fry the sage leaves quickly until they are quite crispy.

Put a bed of fresh, washed spinach leaves on each plate, put the slices of liver on top, and sprinkle over the sage leaves. If you wish, you can sear the meat with a red hot skewer, to decorate.

Variation: Calf's liver can also be broiled, in which case heat the butter, add the sage and spinach, toss lightly and pour around the meat at the last minute.

—— *Opposite* ——

F*egato con Salvia e Spinaci* – broiled calf's liver with sage and spinach.

CHAPTER FIVE

Cheese, Drinks, Desserts and Fruit

The Italians eat a lot of cheese. They also drink a lot of wine, local and young, and it is not unusual for another bottle of wine to be broached to accompany the last of the cheese! I could write a book on both the wines of the Veneto and on the cheeses of Italy. Here I have had to skim over the subjects to give you an initial introduction.

The cheeses of the Veneto

There are said to be some 450 cheeses made in Italy, of which only the most famous – Parmesan, Gorgonzola, Dolcelatte and Bel Paese – are known to any extent abroad. One of the principal reasons is that many of the local cheeses are very soft, made to be eaten within a day, which means that they would not travel. The majority of cheeses native to the Veneto are of this nature, and are made daily in the *latteria* (dairy) in every small town or on the farm. They are very creamy, very fresh and very beautiful.

Most of these soft cheeses are made with cow's milk from the

animals grazing on the rich pasture of the Veneto (although goats' and sheep's milk cheeses are also found). They are sometimes used in cooking, but mostly they are eaten during a meal, between the salad or main course and the fruit or dessert. Often a simple family lunch could consist solely of a salad and cheese. They are eaten with delicious crusty Italian bread, but without butter as they are so creamy; or they are accompanied by fruit – a pear or an apple – or a salad vegetable such as celery. I like to season these *latteria* cheeses with a little salt and pepper and a touch of extra virgin olive oil on the top.

Mascarpone is a soft cow's milk cheese, almost like very thick double cream, and it is used in the making of Tiramisù (see page 185). It was originally from Lombardy rather than from the Veneto itself, and it is becoming more commonly available outside Italy. The other soft cheese used in my recipes is *Ricotta*, now produced commercially all over Italy. It is really a by-product of cheese, as it is made from the whey of *Mozzarella*, *Provolone* and other cheeses. It can be used in sweet dishes, but is perfect for *tortelloni* and other stuffed pasta and pancakes.

A semi-soft cheese, *Montasio*, is perhaps the best known named cheese in the Veneto. It is eaten as a table cheese after two months, but can also be used grated in cooking when it is older. The semi-soft cheese I've used in one of my recipes is *Fontina*, a northern Italian cheese known in Italy since the fifteenth century. It is the best Italian cooking cheese, along with Parmesan, and if not available can be replaced with Gouda.

The third category of Italian cheeses according to consistency is the very hard or grating cheese, *grana*. Parmigiano-Reggiano or Parmesan is

Previous page

A huge variety of cheeses are available in Italy –
and this is just one local shop in the Treviso area.

obviously the best known, and this is used a great deal, grated, in all Italian cooking. It is also delicious served in chunks after dinner, accompanied simply by a glass of good red wine and perhaps some nuts. Another *grana*, the *Grana Padano*, is made in many regions, including the Veneto. *Asiago* is a cow's milk cheese made near Vicenza, and is available as a hard grating cheese and as a softer table cheese.

Wines of the Veneto

The Veneto is one of the major wine-producing areas of Italy, and myriad grape varieties contribute to a vast selection of wines. It is said that Italy produces more wine than any other country, except France, but this is primarily due to the fact that a majority of local grapes are made into local wines for local consumption. These can be less than superb, but are always well worth trying when you are visiting the area.

Even in restaurants, Italians seem rarely to ask for a special wine; they drink the house wine, *vino de la casa*, asking simply for *rosso* or *blanco*, red or white. Often these wines will not even have been bottled – they're usually rather young – and a white might not have been chilled. A special restaurant could have a selection of more special wines, but these types of restaurant are rather few and far between. Even at home, there will simply be a big bottle of wine on the table which many would dilute with water. Wine, to many Italians, is almost an extension of water, merely something to drink with a meal.

However, the situation is getting better, and the good wines – of which there are a considerable number – are becoming more widely

Overleaf
The sloping vineyards in the Soligo area
where the grapes are grown for the famous Venetian *Prosecco*.

available; wines are being kept more conscientiously; and restaurants are beginning to pay more attention to their wine lists. If Italy has been producing *quantity* wine for decades, it has only started producing *quality* wines in the last 20 years. In general terms avoid cheap Italian wine if you don't want to be disappointed – price does reflect quality in this case. If you're ordering in a restaurant and you don't want the house wine, ask for advice.

Among the red wines produced in the Veneto are two of Italy's best-known exports, Valpolicella and Bardolino. The former, when good, can be very good indeed, but it is the name of a *type* of wine, and standards can vary. Of 50 or so Valpolicellas produced, perhaps only five or six could be considered really good. Valpolicella, made from grapes which grow on the foothills rising from the shores of Lake Garda, is soft and dry, slightly fuller than Bardolino, and can be drunk with meats like ham or veal, game and liver. Bardolino is a very light red, one which I could quite happily drink with poultry, but it's also good with the lighter meats like veal. You could drink it with fish too, if you like. Recioto Amarone della Valpolicella – or simply Amarone or Recioto – is a dry, heavy, round-bodied red from near Verona, which is good with game; there is also a sweet sparkling version to drink with desserts.

The Merlot grape is grown all over Italy, but the wine made from it in the Veneto is lighter than elsewhere, and is a good everyday red. The Cabernet is a very serious wine, full-bodied and vigorous, and when it is good, it can easily match, if not outshine, its French counterparts. Raboso is a rough red, drunk young right across the whole region, and Venegazzù is an interesting red to try with meat (the *grappa* from Venegazzù is one of the best).

As for whites, the most famous to come from the Veneto is Soave, and it's one of Italy's finest. (But, like Valpolicella, standards can vary.)

It's dry, and a straw yellow rather than white in color. My favorite white wine is Pinot Grigio which, like another white, Tocai, is made from superb-quality grapes grown in Collio, the part of the Veneto between Venice and Trieste. Both are dry, as are less well known wines – Verduzzo, Vespaiolo and the Chardonnay, which is slightly bubbly on the tongue. All these whites are good with starters, fish or chicken – the Pinot Grigio perhaps more of a main-course wine.

The wine to taste when in Venice, though, is Prosecco, and this is what you should sip as an *ombretta* (little shade) in the cafés and bars throughout the city as you rest your feet. It is slightly sparkling, aromatic and fresh, yellowish in color, and is served in most Venetian restaurants as a house wine. This is also the wine used in Harry's Bar – which must not be missed on a visit to Venice – for making their famous Bellini cocktail, Prosecco with fresh peach juice. Other 'cocktail bars' throughout the world will serve a Bellini at any time of year, made with cheap champagne and bottled peach juice – but go to Harry's Bar at the wrong time and they will look at you as if you're quite mad, and say '*Ma no signore*, there are no peaches *now*.' The alternative offered would depend again on the season: if autumn, you might have a Tiziano, made with the juice of the first crushed red grapes. At other times, you may be given a Tintoretto made with pomegranate juice, a Rossini made with crushed strawberries, or a Mimosa, made with orange juice. All contain the *frizzante* Prosecco.

Aperitivi

When it comes to aperitifs, there are two very famous Venetian concoctions – *aperol* and *select*. *Aperol* is an orange-colored, slightly bitter drink, *select* is similar tasting but browner in colour. Drink either with a

A very Venetian finale to a meal – fresh grapes,
coffee and a glass of Prosecco into which to dip a crisp sweet cake.

dash of soda and a slice of orange or lemon. People meet in bars for
aperitifs in Italy – the busy times are before lunch or in the evening
before going home. Every bar also has its own speciality – ask for
l'aperitivo de la casa. Around Venice people tend to drink wine quite a
lot as an aperitif, particularly *spumante*, sparkling wine.

Digestivi

Italy is the country of aperitifs – there must be some 50 different kinds – but it is also the country of the digestif. There are about 20 different kinds of bitters, *amari* – the most famous are Fernet Branca, Lamozzitti, Averna, Diciotto (18). The most famous of the Italian spirits is *grappa*, a *marc* or brandy distilled from the crushed grapes – pips, skins and all – after the juice has been extracted for wine. The bulk of Italy's *grappa* is produced in Piedmont and the Veneto, and there are as many different *grappas* as there are grape varieties. The Venegazzù *grappa*, for instance, is distilled from Prosecco grapes, and aged in oak casks.

Grappa can be very cheap or very expensive and the market is constantly increasing. *Grappa* has been drunk in people's homes in the Veneto for centuries and it was here it was first produced commercially. Nardini in Bassano del Grappa were the first to produce a world-famous brand. Just as the Royal Navy used to have their daily tot of rum, the Italian *Alpini*, the mountain soldiers, are allowed their daily tot of *grappa*. It's very much a Veneto mountain drink. One of my own first memories goes back to my childhood. Grappa then was much rougher and was used as a natural form of human central heating. In those days I had to get up very early at around five in the morning to get ready for the school bus. I would go down and open up the bar, which was also the local tobacconist. Every day the old peasant women dressed in black, in from the villages to shop for their families, would come first thing for a warming drink. They would down a large glass and say, 'I don't know why men drink this stuff. Give me another glass!' Then they would be off to the next port of call for their shopping – and another bar.

Grappa is not just drunk after a meal, it is the fortification often needed to recharge batteries mid-morning or mid-afternoon. Perhaps it's at its restorative best in coffee – a *caffè corretto* – and this is a fitting link between two famous aspects of Venice: the local grape spirit, and coffee – introduced to Europe by the Venetians, and first drunk in the sixteenth century in the Piazza San Marco!

Dolci (Desserts)

In Italy, desserts are not considered of great importance, either on restaurant menus or in home cooking. A meal is more likely to end with a little fresh fruit. That is not to say that the Italians do not have a sweet tooth, for ever since the Venetians started to import cane sugar from the East, Italians have produced a multitude of sweet cakes and pastries, some of the best in the world. These are produced on the whole, however, by *pasticcerie* (cake shops), from where both domestic and restaurant customers will buy their supplies. The *pasticceria* is always open on Sundays, and it is then that families tend to buy for their special weekend celebratory meal, Sunday lunch. Venetians only use their cars once a week, on Sundays, when they go out for lunch. So if you see a VE number plate, beware! They are known for being dangerous drivers! They flood into the *Terra Ferma* in their hundreds to their favorite lunchtime haunts. Lunch goes on for a minimum of three hours. . . .

One dessert that has become popular – and inevitably so, as the Italians can lay claim to having invented it and introduced it to the rest of Europe – is the *gelato* or ice cream. The technique was brought by the Arabs, and it spread from the south, eventually conquering the world. The best Italian ice cream used to be a seasonal treat, but now it is available commercially all year round. If the quality is not perhaps so superb as it once was, the production is strictly controlled and Italian ice cream and sorbets are still among the best in the world. Most restaurants will offer an ice cream cake, *torta di gelato* or *zuccotto*, for instance, rather than a cake or other dessert, as ice cream is easy to keep and doesn't easily deteriorate.

Conegliano, in the Dolomites, is a town particularly associated with *gelaterie*. From there, many ice cream makers emigrated to Germany to open ice cream parlors (in much the same way and at the same time as other Italians opened Italian restaurants in Britain and America), and one could be forgiven for thinking that Conegliano in the summer was extraordinarily popular with German tourists, judging by the numerous German car number plates. However, they are almost always Italian ice cream makers returning from Germany for their summer holidays!

There are few desserts native to the Veneto, as there has never been a great tradition of cooking with sugar – despite the Venetian historical association – or pastry-making, as in other parts of the country. One exception is the famous Venetian *Tiramisù* – which literally means 'pick-me-up' – a light confection of cream, egg yolks, lady fingers and coffee. It was created about 20 years ago by Alfredo Beltrame, the owner of the El Toulá restaurant in Treviso. You can use whisky, brandy or any other pick-me-up you think you might need!

<h1 style="text-align:center">TIRAMISÙ</h1>

<h3 style="text-align:center">Pick-Me-Up</h3>

SERVES 4
6 egg yolks
sugar to taste
2¼ cups heavy cream or *mascarpone* if you can find it

a dash of whisky, brandy or rum
24 lady fingers
4½ cups strong black coffee, cooled
unsweetened cocoa powder

Beat the egg yolks with a little sugar and mix into the cream or *mascarpone*. Add the (generous) dash of alcohol and beat until fluffy.

The most famous Venetian dessert, *Tiramesù* (page 185) – which originated in the
Veneto – and *fugassa* or *panettone*, the dry cake bought from the *pasticceria*.

Soak the lady fingers briefly in the coffee and use half to line the bottom of a
serving dish. Arrange half the fluffy cream carefully on top, then add another layer of
soaked lady fingers. Cover with the rest of the cream and dust the top lightly with
cocoa. Refrigerate until needed, or serve immediately.

In the Veneto, there are also several variations on the *strudel*, an
Austrian souvenir from the days of the Republic. The only creamy cake I
like – I much prefer the drier Italian cakes – is one called *crema* (an

*G*alani (page 189) – crisp little cakes dusted with confectioners sugar –
are served at Santini after dinner with coffee.

original name, it means cream!) which is made with layers of puff pastry
or *millefoglie*: pastry on the bottom, then a thick custard (*crema
inglese*), then a layer of sponge soaked with a liqueur like Maraschino,
followed by more custard and a little cream, and a final layer of puff
pastry sprinkled with confectioners sugar on top. It's cut in squares, and
is a delicious combination of crunchiness on top and bottom with an
alcoholic softness in the middle. People buy this at the *pasticceria*.

Cakes in the Veneto, though, as elsewhere in Italy, are for special occasions – for birthdays, christenings and weddings. Christmas and Easter demand special cakes too – *fugassa* and *panettone*. At Christmas, lunch used to begin at 12.30 and we would finally stagger up from the table at around 6.30. We would begin with salami and *prosciutto*, then proceed to *riso in brodo fegattini* (broth with rice and chicken livers) and *bollito misto*. After a necessary pause we would begin again with *arrosto misto* (mixed roast meats) accompanied by *mostarda con mascarpone*. After all that came the celebratory *panettone*, home-made in those days, a light, dry sponge flavored with lemon, candied peel and white raisins.

The feast which preceded Easter was one of the big occasions of my childhood years. *Venerdi Santo* – Good Friday – was naturally devoted to fish, with a lunch of six or seven different courses, eventually followed by the simple, dryish *fugassa*. This is the Venetian dialect word for *focaccia*, a bread which can be flavored in a variety of ways – sweet in Venice at Easter. In the run-up to Easter, the Mardi Gras celebrations remain in my memory as well. Every year a group of us children would don masks as is traditional, and go round the houses of our parents claiming wine and cakes. The parents would have to pretend not to recognise any of us while they quizzed us and fed us special crisp little cakes called variously throughout Italy *galani*, *crostoli*, *chiacchere*, *cenci*, and *bugie*. *Galani* is the name for them in Venice, where they are eaten particularly at carnival time. I serve them instead of *petits fours* at my restaurants in London, and they are very popular indeed. They are also eaten in the afternoon, with coffee.

GALANI

◆

6 whole eggs
half their weight in sugar
half their weight in butter
a small glass of *grappa*

a pinch of salt
half the weight of the eggs in all-
    purpose flour
vegetable oil, for frying
confectioners sugar

Beat the eggs and mix with the sugar, butter and *grappa*. Add the salt and begin to add the flour slowly until you have a firm dough.

Roll out thinly on a floured surface and cut into oblongs about 3 inches long. Cut two diagonal slashes in each, so they will puff up during cooking. (The dough can also be cut into ribbons and tied in bows before deep-frying).

Fry in very hot oil until golden, drain on kitchen paper and serve with a dusting of confectioners sugar.

Another deep-fried cake is *frittole*, the Venetian dialect name for *frittelle*, which means fritters. *Frittole* actually means 'carnival' in Venice, and the cakes are rather similar to doughnuts.

FRITTOLE

◆

$3\frac{1}{2}$ cups all-purpose flour
$\frac{1}{2}$ cake compressed yeast, dissolved in
    warm water
generous $\frac{1}{2}$ cup sugar
scant $\frac{1}{2}$ cup white wine, plus a little
    warm water as necessary

grated zest of 1 lemon
$\frac{1}{3}$ cup white raisins
vegetable oil, for frying
confectioners sugar

Mix all the ingredients except for the oil and confectioners sugar together, and beat very well into a smooth batter. Let this rest for 1 hour in a warm, not hot, place.

Put a deep pan of light vegetable oil on to heat and test for temperature by dribbling a little of the batter into it. If it sizzles and turns golden the oil is ready.

*F*ritole (page 189), Venetian sweet cake, as served at Da Lino in Solighetto.
Very good after dinner with a glass of sparkling white Prosecco.

Drop the batter into the oil in spoonfuls, taking care not to overcrowd the pan. When the *frittole* are a nice golden color remove them and drain well on paper towels.

When they are all ready, serve them hot with a light dusting of confectioners sugar.

Bussolai are ring- or S-shaped cookies from Venice, or more particularly Burano, where they are served at Romano's. They are also common in Friuli, the region to the north-east of the Veneto, adjoining Yugoslavia.

Bussolai (page 192) – often called *esse* because of their shape – as prepared at Da Romano in Burano, served with a piece of *croccante*, the Italian version of praline.

Bussolai used to be given to a child by its godparents on confirmation day. Like *zaete* or *zalete*, a cornmeal cookie and another Burano speciality, *bussolai* are served with fruit and coffee, and dipped into the last of the wine.

BUSSOLAI

3½ cups all-purpose flour
2½ cups sugar
9 egg yolks

1 whole egg
a knob of butter
a pinch of salt

Beat everything together to form a dough. Roll out on to a floured surface and cut into strips about the size of your finger. Form these into 'S' shapes or rings and place on a greased cookie sheet. Cook in a medium oven at 350°F until nicely browned, then allow to cool.

These little biscuits are traditional, and may be found in many of the local *pasticcerie*. They can be flavored by any liqueur – a citron one, for instance – but the cherry liqueur made in the Veneto is particularly apt.

BISCOTTI ALLA VENEZIANA

Venetian Biscuits

5 eggs, separated
generous ½ cup superfine sugar
1 cup all-purpose flour

a pinch of salt
½ tablespoon Maraschino Liqueur
confectioners sugar

Beat the egg yolks and sugar together in a bowl until white and creamy. Fold in the flour and salt and mix gently.

Beat the egg whites until stiff and fold in along with the Maraschino. Place carefully in a piping bag.

Pipe lengths of about 3 inches on to cookie sheets covered with good baking parchment. Bake in a preheated oven at 350°F. Leave to cool, and when completely cold dust with confectioners sugar.

Frutta (Fruit)

Fresh fruit is still the most popular everyday finale to an Italian or Venetian meal, and there is fruit in abundance in the Veneto. Jesolo, for instance, has some of the largest *frutteti* (orchards) in Italy, and supplies apples, pears, cherries and peaches to the whole country. (I well remember 'relieving' trees of their fruit as a boy, and being chased, caught and chastised. . . .) What cannot be grown locally – lemons, oranges and other fruits which need the full force of the more southerly sun – are simply brought north. One of the special taste treats of my childhood, for instance, was a stick of licorice poked through the thick skin into the flesh of an 'imported' *cedro* or citron. (When older, I tended to appreciate more the taste of the drink made from citron, *cedrata*!)

Fruit used to be strictly seasonal in Veneto, like everywhere else, although it is less so now. But we still enjoy the traditional fruits in season: nuts, pears, oranges and tangerines in winter; peaches, apricots, cherries and grapes and so on in summer. One of the major summer pleasures in the Veneto is watermelon – the best in Europe – which are cultivated on the sunny sides of houses and gardens, and ripened until nearly burned by the sun. When cut, you can almost see the fruit sugar

——— *Overleaf* ———

A wonderful display of fresh fruit,
to be served as dessert, in a typical Venetian restaurant.

193

next to the skin. Melons, too, were first cultivated in Italy on a large scale, and because the *cantelupo* (or canteloupe) is so much associated with Italy, it wasn't until I went to London that I realised there were other varieties available. As well as being eaten as desserts, a *cantelupo* is the best – to me the *only* – melon to serve with *prosciutto* or Parma ham; they can also take a light sprinkling of some Parmesan which, with other melons, would be like serving cheese on top of chocolate cake!

Pears and figs can also be served with Parma ham, and we use a lot of figs in season, in August and September. The trouble with figs – and with *kaki*, a variety of persimmon – is that they grow so profusely (often in the wild) that there is a glut, and one can easily get very fed up with the fruit! However, a bowl of fresh figs on the table – not stewed or presented artistically in a pool of raspberry *coulis* – is one of the year's delights. In fact, the only concession we in the Veneto, whether at home or in a restaurant, would make to dessert presentation is in the form of a fresh fruit salad – a mixture of the beautiful fresh fruits abundantly available to us. There might also be a *misto bosco*, a combination of several kinds of wild berries, including strawberries or blackberries picked from the local woods, dressed with lemon juice, some sugar and a little gin.

One of the major fruits of the Veneto is, of course, the grape, for the Veneto is a major wine-producing area of Italy. There is an enormous variety of grapes available for the wines are many – Valpolicella, Soave, Bardolino, Tocai, Merlot, Cabernet, Prosecco, Pinot Grigio and so on (see page 181). Each September, there is a grape festival in Jesolo, when every farmer organizes a sort of carnival procession in which people follow the tractor and grapes are given away.

Cherries are grown in abundance here, and a very famous variety in the Veneto is the *marosticane*. This is a big red and white cherry which is very crunchy. The town that bears the same name is famous for another reason: they play live chess there in the square. Another variety is the *amarena* cherry – also known as *amarasca* – which is made into the liqueur Maraschino. These cherries have a bitter flavor and are not often eaten fresh, but are preserved in alcohol or made into sorbets and ice cream. The area where Maraschino was originally made – Zara, in Dalmatia – became part of Yugoslavia after the Second World War, and the family who manufactured the liqueur moved back into northern Italy to continue production.

Italy is now a major producer of the kiwi fruit, and the industry was started by a famous Italian actor, Fabio Testi, near Verona. Another fruit is the medlar, a member of the Rosaceae family like the apple, pear, quince and loquat. Loquats can be eaten fresh from the tree, but medlars need to be 'bletted' or left until very soft, almost rotted, before they can be eaten. There is a saying in Italy that time under straw will mature the medlar (ie, that patience is required) – *'Il tempo e la paglia maturano le nespole.'* Pomegranates are in season in October and November, and it is then that Paeta al Malgaragno – turkey with pomegranate – is prepared. The pomegranate juice and crushed seeds are added half-way through the cooking and used to baste the bird.

Nuts, too, are grown in the Veneto and I can remember, just after the war, buying little bags of chestnut flour into which you would dip your licked finger as if it were sherbet. There was a tradition – I hope it still exists – of going into the country on the day of San Martino in November to eat roasted sweet chestnuts (*marrone*) along with the new wine – which at that stage was very sweet and very cloudy. Although chestnuts are used a lot in the cuisine of neighbouring regions, they do not feature much in recipes from the Veneto. Almonds do, however, in a praline-like sweet called *croccante*.

In the countryside of the Veneto, a lot of the fruit abundance would be preserved. Nothing elaborate: a preserving jar, a bottle of cheap *grappa*, a fruit – big grapes, cherries, apricots, peaches, prunes or white raisins – and some sugar to taste. At the end of 4 months, the fruit will be soft and can be eaten in winter as a rather alcoholic dessert. The *grappa* itself benefits too. I like grapes best, but you have to be very careful about choosing the fruit: they must be very mature, almost transparent, but still crunchy, when they will be sweet and good. I always leave a tiny piece of the stalk on each grape otherwise the puncture left by its removal will turn brown.

A selection of cheeses – *Dolcelatte*, *Provolone*, *Parmigiano* – with a bottle of Chianti, selected fresh fruits and sliced *panforte*.

Seasonal Menus

Planning of menus should always be done according to the season, and the availability of fresh produce. And you should never really plan a menu until you have *seen* what is fresh and available. It would be unwise, for instance, to try to make a *funghi porcini* dish in early summer (they're available dried, of course, but not really so good), or an asparagus *risotto* in September. Asparagus *is* available, of course, but it's imported from across the Atlantic, is not nearly so tasty as home grown, and it's often prohibitively expensive.

Thus, I have given a few ideas for *seasonal* dishes using seasonal foods, and ones that are appropriate to the weather. I've also given alternative types of meal: a light lunch or a more substantial dinner (or vice versa, of course!).

SPRING

Fiori di Zucchini Ripieni
(Stuffed Zucchini Flowers)
page 92

Scaloppine al Limone
(Veal Scallops with Lemon)
page 158

Cooked vegetables of choice or side salad

Carciofi Santini
(Braised Artichokes)
page 93

Pappardelle con Carciofi
(Ribbon Pasta with Artichoke Sauce)
page 53

Salmone Santini
(Salmon with Peppercorns)
page 135

Side salad

Dessert or fresh fruit of choice

Tagliolini con Pomodoro e Basilico
(*Tagliolini* with Tomatoes and Basil)
page 51

or

Risotto Primavera
(*Risotto* with Young Spring Vegetables)
page 72

Pollo Santini
(Chicken Breast with Mustard)
page 141

Cooked vegetables of choice

Fresh fruit in season

SUMMER

Spiedini di Gamberoni
(Shrimp Brochettes)
page 117

Risotto con Zucchini
(Zucchini *Risotto*)
page 73

Side salad

Fresh fruit

Sardine in Saor
(Sweet and Sour Sardines)
page 119

or

Insalata di Mare
(Seafood Salad)
page 120

Spaghetti alle Vongole
(Spaghetti with Fresh Clams)
page 57

Branzino Santini
(Sea Bass with Herb Sauce)
page 133

Boiled vegetables
(potatoes, zucchini)
and a green side salad

Fruit salad
or
Tiramisù
(Pick-Me-Up)
page 185

Zuppa di Cozze
(Mussel Soup)
page 114

*Spaghetti con
Melanzane e Olive*
(Spaghetti with
Eggplant and Olives)
page 56

Side salad

Cheese or fruit

AUTUMN

Funghi con Polenta
(Wild Mushrooms with *Polenta*)
page 104

Quaglie con Funghi
(Quail with Mushrooms)
page 146

Vegetables of choice

Fruit or cheese

Tagliolini con Funghi
(*Tagliolini* with Mushrooms)
page 51

Faraona con la Peverada
(Guinea Hen with Pepper Sauce)
page 152

Vegetables of choice

Fruit

Cappe Sante
(Baked Scallops)
page 124

Gnocchi Verdi con Gorgonzola
(Spinach *Gnocchi* with Gorgonzola)
page 65

Galletto alla Diavola
(Grilled Small
Broiling Chicken)
page 141

Side salad

Fruit

WINTER

Pasta e Fagioli
(Pasta and Bean Soup)
page 89

Pollo in Tecia
(Chicken with Mushrooms
and Tomatoes)
page 144

Polenta
page 102

Side Salad

Fruit

Sopa Coada
(Squab Soup)
page 151

Anatra al Forno
(Duck with Anchovy Sauce)
page 149

Vegetables of choice

Fruit

Radicchio alla Griglia
(Broiled Radicchio)
page 96

Risotto con Fegattini
(Chicken Liver Risotto)
page 74

Rognoni Trifolati
(Sautéed Kidneys)
page 168

Side salad

Fruit

Afterword

If I've been able to enthuse you about Venice and the Veneto, made you aware of the pleasures that could await you, when would be the best time to go? Obviously not in the high summer, when Venice disappears beneath a sea of tourists and the canals turn rank in the heat, but the spring, when the countryside bursts into life, or the autumn, when the mist swirls up from the lagoon, are both marvellous. At both these times, you'll be able to enjoy seasonal specialities. *Risi e Bisi* in spring, for instance, and the *funghi* dishes in autumn. If you're incurably romantic you might consider the depths of winter, but be warned, you'll need warm underwear and gumboots (not very romantic) because the weather is bitterly cold and the canals flood every year. If it snows you'll edge along clinging to buildings, scared you're just about to slide into the canal, while tiny, black-clad Venetian ladies of great age skip along, nimble as mountain goats. Then you'll appreciate the sterling qualities of *polenta* and Pasta e Fagioli and all the other good, warming and filling dishes for which the area is famous.

Venice is so popular and so firmly on the tourist map that one forgets it has a real life of its own: the sight of a crane, or a tree growing in the middle of a little square, can come as a shock, an intrusion from the outside world. You are reminded that this isn't a floating dream-city built by one eccentric and peopled by others – the Venetians regard this as the normal world and everything out there with its streets, cars and factories as quite unnatural. And do stop to consider that there are people living on Burano and Torcello who may never have left the island once in their lives, not even to visit the big city. . . .

For those readers who actually want to experience fabulous Venetian food when visiting the city and the surrounding area, I can recommend the following:

''al graspa de ua''
Calle dei Bombaseri, 5094
30124 Venezia
Tel. 041.700150/5223647

Trattoria Do Forni
calle dei Specchieri 457/468
30124 Venezia
Tel. 041.5237729

Trattoria Alla Madonna
calla della Madonna
Rialto
30124 Venezia
Tel. 041.5223824

Harry's Bar
calle Vallaresso 1323
30124 Venezia
Tel. 041.5236797

Trattoria Da Romano
Via Galuppi 221
Burano (VE)
Tel. 041.730030

Ostaria al Ponte del Diavolo
Torcello (VE)
Tel. 041.730401

Gambrinus
San Polo di Piave
31020 Treviso
Tel. 0422.742043

Relais El Toula
Paderno di Ponzano
31020 Treviso
Tel. 0422.969023

Alfredo – Relais el Toula
via Collalto 26
31020 Treviso
Tel. 0422.540275

Al Bersagliere
via Barberia 21
31020 Treviso
Tel. 0422.541988

Albergo Ristorante Beccherie
piazza Ancillotto 10
31020 Treviso
Tel.0422.540871

Ristorante al Salisa
via XX Settembre 2
31015 Conegliano (TV)
Tel. 0438.24288

Da Lino
Locanda Ristorante
via Brandolini 31
31050 Solighetto di Pieve di Soligo (TV)
Tel. 0438.82150/82856

Ristorante Da Gigetto
via A. De Gaspari 4
31050 Maine (TV)
Tel. 0438.893126

Guaiane
Noventa di Piave
30020 (VE)
Tel.0421.65002

Alla Colonna
Via Campana 27
31100 Treviso
Tel. 0422.544804

Recipe Index

205

General Index